THE DOG ALLUSION

Martin Rowson is an award-winning political cartoonist whose work appears regularly in the *Guardian*, the *Independent on Sunday*, the *Daily Mirror*, the *Scotsman*, the *Spectator*, the *Morning Star*, *Tribune*, *Index on Censorship* and *The New Humanist*. His previous publications include comic-book adaptations of *The Waste Land* and *Tristram Shandy*, and with Cape and Vintage a novel, *Snatches*, and a memoir, *Stuff*. *Fuck: The Human Odyssey* will be published by Cape in October 2008. Martin Rowson is a former vice-president of the Zoological Society of London, a trustee of the Powell-Cotton Natural History Museum and an honorary associate of the National Secular Society. He lives with his wife and their two teenage children in south-east London.

ALSO BY MARTIN ROWSON

MARTIN ROWSON

The Dog Allusion

Pets, Gods and How to be Human

VINTAGE BOOKS
London

Published by Vintage 2008

2 4 6 8 10 9 7 5 3 1

Vintage
Random House, 20 Vauxhall Bridge Road,
London SW1V 2SA

www.vintage-books.co.uk

Addresses for companies within The Random House Group Limited
can be found at: www.randomhouse.co.uk/offices.htm

The Random House Group Limited Reg. No. 954009

A CIP catalogue record for this book
is available from the British Library

ISBN 9780099521334

The Random House Group Limited supports The Forest Stewardship
Council (FSC), the leading international forest certification
organisation. All our titles that are printed on Greenpeace approved
FSC certified paper carry the FSC logo. Our paper procurement
policy can be found at www.rbooks.co.uk/environment

Typeset by SX Composing DTP, Rayleigh, Essex
Printed and bound in Great Britain by
CPI Cox & Wyman, Reading RG1 8EX

For Basil, Ginger and Pansy,
and in loving memory of Sybil, Fosco, Templeton, Snowy,
Snowy II, Mandy-moo-moo and the rest of them,
all of whom died without receiving last rites.

Introduction

What follows is a considerably expanded version of a talk I originally gave on 15 March 2007 at a meeting of the Lewisham Humanist Group in an upper room at The Goose public house in Catford, South-East London. It's a pretty rough pub, but upstairs sat a small group of nice, kind, rather elderly people, numbering only slightly more than those who attended Jesus Christ's Last Supper.

The talk went down pretty well, even though I spoke for over an hour, and I suspect that they were expecting something more in line with my day job as a political cartoonist. The next day I emailed my script to my agent David Miller, a theology graduate with whom I've discussed religion and atheism at length since he first took me on in the summer of 2004. Despite his training, some of it at the hands of the former Dean of Trinity – the Very Reverend John Bowker – who once defined religions in the contemporary world as 'licenced insanities', Miller and I are pretty much of one mind as far as God is concerned. Given the current trend for books on the subject, he therefore sent the script to Dan Franklin at Jonathan Cape. Dan's already published two other books of mine, and he passed the script on to his colleagues at Vintage.

That, in short, is the genesis of what you now have in your hands.

A month or so after Vintage had bought the idea, I was whoring one of those previous books at a literary festival, this being the service which is perfect freedom that all modern authors now enjoy or endure. Right at the end of the session someone asked what I was going to do next, so I answered that I was writing my God book, because everybody now had to write a God book. Mine, however, was at least in part taking a whack at Richard Dawkins and Christopher Hitchens as well as God. But as I was trying to articulate this, being only human I got slightly tongue-tied and Dawkins and Hitchens came out as 'Hawkins and Ditchens'.

I liked that. The names suggested to me a firm of slightly old-fashioned gentlemen's outfitters in somewhere like Ludlow, working away in their low-ceilinged, oak-panelled shop, with Hawkins, the more serious and senior of the partners, rolling out the yards and yards of sober, serious, tough and impermeable cloth. And Ditchens, rather shakily, would then cut the cloth to suit whatever his mood happened to be that day.

That said, as there now seems to be a priesthood of all unbelievers, and if a geneticist and a journalist can encroach territory outside their specific areas of expertise and have their say about religion, then it's high time the satirists and cartoonists got in on the act too.

However, apart from the title, this book isn't a satire, although I hope you'll find parts of it funny. Nor is it a work of scholarship, because I'm no scholar. Nor am I a geneticist, a scientist, theologian, philosopher or anything else that might qualify me to add my bit to the ongoing and largely bogus debate between religion and atheism. I am, however, human like the rest of us, and the human element is something which has, so far, been conspicuously missing from the volleys fired by both sides.

Although this isn't a work of scholarship (there's no index, for a start), it is the result of me absorbing the thoughts and ideas of many other people, as you'll probably notice, although I don't think this particular synthesis of those ideas has been presented in quite this way before. If it has, I can only apologise and make an insincere promise to widen my reading. The book's also meant to be playful, rude, sweepingly generalising, discursive and often digressive, as well as serious. This is an approach which I think fits the subject perfectly.

Finally, while not wishing further to try your patience before the main attraction, I'd like to thank the following people: Denis Cobell and everyone at the Lewisham Humanist Group for their hospitality and patience; David Miller and Hannah Westland at Rogers, Coleridge and White; my editors Ros Porter and Frances MacMillan at Vintage and everyone else at Random House who helped in the production of this book; Francis Wheen; Rosemary and James Furber; Malcolm Guite; the late Dr Robert Buttimore; Neil and Martin Simpson; Posy Simmonds; Laurie Taylor; Caspar Melville of *New Humanist* and Chris McLaughlin of *Tribune*, in whose pages some of the ideas in this book first appeared; my wife Anna Clarke and our children Fred and Rose Rowson; Rory Hodgson; and finally, obviously, my pets, who made no contribution to it whatsoever, beyond the central role I describe for them in the main body of the text.

There isn't an index, and there isn't a bibliography either. However, it seems to be obligatory in other books like this to burden the reader with further reading, so I'll recommend the following books which are germane in part to parts of my argument, and also worth reading in their own right when you get bored with this one. They are: *In the Company of Animals* by James Serpell; *The Last Revolution: 1688 and the Creation of the Modern World*, by Patrick Dillon; *A Revolutionary Rogue: Henry Marten and the English Republic* by Sarah Barber; *Fatal Purity: Robespierre and the French Revolution* by Ruth Scurr; *Slaughterhouse 5* by Kurt Vonnegut Jnr (if only for the reference to Kilgor Trout's science fiction story about the crucifixion); and *My Last Breath* by Luis Buñuel. I also strongly recommend that you watch the first *Alien* film, which ably demonstrates the lengths we'll go to on behalf of our pets when Ripley returns to the mother ship even though it's about to explode, to save Jones, the ship's cat.

In the end, I found no room in the book to include a story from *My Last Breath*, which shows how the latest row between religion and secularism is nothing new. It's about the anticlerical newspaper one of the local gentry owned when Buñuel was a child in rural Spain in the 1900s, which once described how four worker comrades were walking down the street when they saw a priest coming in the other direction. The report concluded thus: 'Faced with this overwhelming provocation, they beat him to within an inch of his life.'

Pax vobiscum.

Martin Rowson, Lewisham, Hallowe'en 2007

empathy *em'pe-thi, n.* the power of entering into another's personality and imaginatively experiencing his experiences: the power of entering into the feeling or spirit of something and so appreciating it fully.

Chambers Twentieth Century Dictionary

For what man in the natural state or course of thinking, did ever conceive it in his power to reduce the notions of all mankind exactly to the same length, and breadth, and height as his own?

Jonathan Swift, from 'A Digression on Madness'
in *A Tale of a Tub*, 1704

Never obey orders, including this one.

Dr K. E. K. Rowson, MD, PhD, MRCS, LRCP, MB,
B.Chir., Dip.Bact. and MRCPath, mid 1970s.

There is a particular human activity or trait with which I think we're all familiar. It is common to all human societies, and its ubiquity and universality might even lead us to assume that its very existence helps define what we actually mean by the term 'human'. It entails accounting to non- or, if you prefer, extra-human beings or entities a central and possibly pivotal role in human affairs. It also requires from us levels of commitment, attention, expenditure and devotion out of all proportion to the apparent benefits paid back to us in return.

Throughout History it has impelled us to channel precious resources, perhaps better directed towards our own well-being, into husbanding food, building massive edifices, creating entire industries as well as whole classes or castes of highly trained people whose sole function is to service and, indeed, venerate and propitiate this non- or extra-human phenomenon.

With depressing frequency this veneration and propitiation has led to unparalleled levels of callousness or cruelty, not least towards other people. And yet, not just frequently but usually, its subscribers claim that their veneration is actively good for them, and will therefore be good for everyone else as well. They argue that, if only the unconvinced would follow the example of their veneration, they too would become physically, mentally, morally and, dare I say it, spiritually healthier. And it follows from that

that they'll be better people as a consequence. Moreover, the devotees claim that their devotions are capable of transporting them to what can only be described as transcendental heights of complete, unquestioning and unfettered love. This is despite the fact that we are in no more of a position today than we've ever been to judge whether or not any of the attention or expenditure or veneration or propitiation or, indeed, love is reciprocated in any way whatsoever.

Objectively – rationally – the whole enterprise is a monumental and more than faintly ridiculous waste of time, money and energy. Rationally, we should abandon these practices forthwith, along with our deluded faith or trust in their efficacy, and instead concentrate our energies more profitably, sensibly, reasonably and humanely on our fellow human beings rather than continuing to make embarrassing fools of ourselves in the eyes of those wiser people who fail to share our faith.

And yet we persist. Worse, we become shrill and sometimes irrationally violent in insisting not only on our right to persist, but on the absolute rectitude in doing so, even in the face of all reason and common sense.

Just in case you're wondering, I'm talking here about the universal human trait of keeping pets.

There is a wealth of evidence to show that every human society has kept pets, those companion animals who coexist with humans for reasons beyond the rationally explicable purposes of protection, transportation, improved pastoral practices, vermin control or food. And we keep them, despite their rapacious appetites, their capriciousness, fickleness, cynical greed, capacity for random and uncontrolled violence and, of course, the vast amounts of uncompostable shit they produce. We do this because we love them.

Hunter-gatherers in the Amazon keep the orphans of their prey, just for company. The same imperative governs rich little old ladies on the Upper East Side of Manhattan to make them keep tiny dogs in tiny apartments and dress them up in designer clothes. Shortly before fleeing from the advancing forces of the US Army and the Afghan Northern Alliance on a motorbike, the Taliban leader Mullah Omar spent a comforting hour communing with his cats in his garden in Kandahar. President George W. Bush has a pet Scottie dog called Barney; his predecessor, Bill Clinton, had a pet cat called Socks; Hitler had a pet Alsatian called Blondie; Friedrich Engels had a pet hedgehog called, rather prosaically, Hedgehog, which he had stuffed after its death. André Breton, often referred to as 'The Surrealist Pope', told the atheist film director Luis Buñuel that when he was collaborating with Leon Trotsky on their manifesto *Towards a Free Revolutionary Art*, he was disgusted one day to discover his co-author fawning over a small Pomeranian dog. Buñuel, for his part, maintained coteries of rats, mice and lizards for most of his life. The Mayor of London, Ken Livingstone, famously keeps pet newts, and aged eighteen applied for a job as a keeper at London Zoo, although they happened not to be recruiting new staff that year. Gary Bennett, author of the infamous *Crockford's* preface attacking the Archbishop of Canterbury at the time, killed Tibbles, his cat, before sitting in his garaged car and filling it with exhaust fumes.

And although former British Prime Minister Tony Blair notoriously exiled Humphrey the cat from Downing Street, his predecessor Winston Churchill would work most mornings in bed, surrounded by cats and dogs, and Churchill's latest successor Gordon Brown has welcomed his Chancellor Alistair Darling's cat Sybil into Number 10, amidst considerable media interest and much public jubilation.

Archbishop William Laud, who was executed in 1645 during the English Civil War, had a pet tortoise (along with many other pets) which survived its master's beheading by over a hundred years until trodden on by a careless gardener in the middle of the eighteenth century. Prince Rupert of the Rhine, on the same side as Laud in the Civil War, had a poodle called Boy who was killed by a Parliamentarian soldier during the Battle of Marston Moor on 2 July 1644. Pope Leo X yearned to own a pet rhinoceros. Hermann Goering had a pet lion. Lord Byron kept a pet bear with him in his rooms in Cambridge, and his immediate predecessor, the 5th Baron Byron, had a pet wolf. The Pre-Raphaelite poet and painter Dante Gabriel Rossetti kept a menagerie of animals in his garden in Cheyne Walk in Chelsea, including wallabies, wombats and a Brahmin bull: he claimed its eyes reminded him of his mistress and model Jane Morris. King Henry III of England had a pet polar bear, a gift from the King of Norway, which he kept in the Royal Menagerie in the Tower of London and which went for a swim in the River Thames every morning on the end of a length of rope. The French Symbolist poet Gérard de Nerval had a pet lobster which he'd take for walks on a lead along the Bois de Boulogne, explaining to anyone who asked that it 'doesn't bark and knows the Secrets of the Sea'. And as a child I owned a record by Jimmie Rodgers called 'A Little Dog Cried', a deeply respectful and apparently unironic composition all about Jesus Christ's pet dog. It concluded, accompanied by the soaring cadences of a choir of heavenly voices, with the lines, 'A little dog cried when his master died/On a hill a long time ago.' (See Appendix A.) As the atheist writer George Eliot put it so succinctly, 'Animals are such agreeable friends – they ask no questions, they pass no criticisms.'

All sorts of reasons have been given to explain why we keep pets. The Austrian zoologist and animal psychologist

Konrad Lorenz long ago suggested that we keep cats and dogs because of their binocular vision, their large, liquid eyes placed on the front of their soft, round faces reminding us irresistibly of human babies. And yet people also keep rabbits and guinea pigs and mice and hamsters and gerbils whose eyes, stuck on the sides of their empty heads the better to alert them to the presence of potential predators, mark them down in any sensible carnivore's or omnivore's mind as nothing more than food. Yet, by and large, we don't eat them. And in our pet-keeping habits, we stretch the companionship of shared morphology to breaking point. Many of us keep birds and fish and reptiles and amphibians and insects and arachnids, and although we might be tempted to assume some kind of interactivity of companionship between ourselves and our mammalian pets, even if we account the budgies and the guppies and the stick insects with some kind of consciousness, the further down the taxa you go that consciousness becomes so wildly different from our own (we imagine) that any mutually fulfilling meeting of minds becomes hopelessly out of the question.

And yet there they are, in their hundreds of millions, throughout the world and throughout History. And we love them.

Even though some of you might find the following confession deeply nauseating, I happily concede that I love them too. Several years ago, a week after my stepmother had died only a few months after my father's death, we felt obliged to have our seventeen-year-old cat Sybil put to sleep. I loved Sybil deeply, and became convinced, in her later years, that a particular vocalisation she'd developed on entering a room – it sounded something like 'Gneee-yow!' – was her attempt to say 'hello' in human speech, although this conviction on my part was probably entirely irrational. With most of her internal organs close to complete collapse, she sat on my lap as she received the lethal injection from our local vet, and her last actions on earth were to bite me and then piss in my lap. This, I feel, is what she would have wanted.

The grief I felt for Sybil may have been displacement for the grief I was already feeling for my late parents, but it was genuine nonetheless. So was the untrammelled joy I felt when we acquired a new cat called Basil a couple of months later. Again, this might just be a symptom of the kind of emotional bipolarism we all experience during grief, and I admit that I was almost embarrassed by the depths of my elation, and how the presence of this animal unquestionably improved the quality of my life, despite the ever-increasing quarry of legless yet living frogs, headless pigeons and, latterly, throatless squirrels which we have to clear from the house as a consequence. But irrespective of my state of mind when Basil arrived, it also remains a fact that I get an enormous amount of pleasure out of simply observing the shape of a cat's back when it's sitting down, although I can conceive of no evolutionary advantage or theological imperative that should make this so.

As I say, for whatever reason, we love our pets. A lot of us love them much more than we love other people, and some of us may even love them more than we love the god or gods we profess to love. But the real point of all this is that, although it's often not true of other people, in the case of pets and gods, we invariably think that they love us back.

I'm not just making a cheap rhetorical point here, another bit of satirical casuistry the better to whack religion by saying that religion is exactly the same as keeping a pet. And although that is, in fact, precisely what I am saying, it's not purely to get a cheap laugh.

To provide some background here, let me take you back to a party my wife and I went to a few years ago near where we live in South-East London. The party was being thrown by some very good friends of ours who I'd forgotten were also sincere and regular communicants of the Church of England. I'd forgotten this because I choose not to choose the people I like on liturgical, ideological or Manichean grounds alone. Anyway, because I'd forgotten about their faith, I also forgot that most of their other guests were likely to share their beliefs.

I wised up to the situation during a conversation about Rowan Williams, whose translation to the See of Canterbury had just been announced. I was saying that Williams seemed to me to be an inspired choice: he was, after all, a *Guardian*-reading bearded liberal intellectual and I said that his only fault, as far as I could tell, was that he appeared to believe in God.

My joke fell incredibly flat. I was greeted with the same look of slight disgust, mingled with contempt and pity, that I used to get when I'd bad-mouth Margaret Thatcher to right-wing journalist friends in the 1980s, or mentioned smoking a joint to an elderly aunt when I was a teenager.

At this point, to compound my discomfort and, I suspect, to spice things up yet further, my hostess brought over her local vicar and introduced me as the Atheist At The Party. The vicar – wearing a collar and tie and a tweed jacket, all the better to entrap the unwary – looked me up and down and then leant back with a contemptuous and patronising smile and asked me, as an atheist, how I explained the fact that religion was a universal phenomenon in all human societies. Quick as a flash, and without ever really having thought about it before, I asked *him* how he could explain exactly the same thing about keeping pets.

You won't be surprised to hear that he had no answer to that, so we'll assume that I won this latest little joust in the apparently unending battle between religion and secularism. On points, at least. And yet, as I've already said, I wasn't simply bandying about some snappy repartee.

To see why, let's backtrack and reflect for a moment on what it is that actually defines us as human. And while neither religion nor keeping pets exclusively define our humanity, both of them are aspects, or at least consequences, of what does.

By this late stage in the frequently sordid history of our species we're fast running out of those attributes we could once claim marked us uniquely apart from all the other species with whom we uneasily share this planet.

We used to think that we alone had mastered the use of tools, but it's now clear that many other species, including so-called 'lowly' invertebrates like octopuses, do so too, and must have done so for much longer than we have. Bipedalism is obviously out, because it's commonplace. Our facility for opposing our thumbs and forefingers used to be claimed as one of the definingly exclusive badges of our exceptional otherness, because it enabled our use of tools, although several species of bird use their beaks just as effectively. (Being able to play the piano, knit or build Auschwitz is not an explanation of what makes us human but a by-product.) Our brains are, it's true, proportionately quite big, but by no means the biggest, and returning to tools, crows use them and their brains are tiny. Other animals laugh. Nor, to look on the dark side, is our capacity for mindless cruelty or warfare unique to us.

Language, of course, has long been thought to be the defining human quality, but I'm not so sure. I believe it's becoming increasingly clear that what differences there are are simply quantitative: our wide vocabulary of spoken language appears to be massively more sophisticated than the observable vocal, visual or, for that matter, chemical languages of other animals or, indeed, plants. But its power to impart information is, I'd suggest, probably matched in different if currently less understandable but equally effective ways. A limpet periodically squirting pheromones into the surrounding seawater is a limpet's way of saying all it probably needs to say to any other limpet who's interested. (To argue that a limpet is unable to communicate in the same way as us, by squirting a pheromonal transliteration of *Hamlet*, *The Book of Common Prayer*, the Qur'an or *The God Delusion*, is to miss the point entirely. By and large limpets don't need to communicate such things, whereas we do, though not necessarily for the reasons you might think.) Then, of course, there's consciousness, of which language, depending on who you listen to, is either a consequence or the source.

Human consciousness has kept the philosophers guessing for at least the last two and a half millennia, and everyone else for probably as long as we've been here as a species. We're still no closer to understanding precisely what it is or where it comes from or how it works. In the porridge of electrical charges and discharges in our brains, somehow or other is produced our sense of self and self-awareness, that inner voice that lets us recognise who we are and how we relate to everything in the world around us. Whatever this thing is, one consequence of it is our sense of our personal, individual uniqueness, an awareness which is also affected by cultural and environmental factors. Another consequence is our species' singular self-obsession, which in turn has led us up an infinity of teleological blind alleys. For my money, one of the worst of these was thought up by René Descartes, famous for his dictum '*cogito, ergo sum*', 'I think, therefore I am'. Apart from that being an open invitation to collapse in on yourself to the point of solipsism, his theories about the interface between the material and the 'spiritual' – he located the physical point of interface in the pineal gland in the brain – led him to the proposition that other animals, denied a soul, were unable to think except in an entirely instinctive way and are therefore little more than preprogrammed automata. Descartes was also a mathematician, whose (albeit theologically influenced) proto-rationalism lent his opinions a credibility of a kind we'll encounter later, and gave a further respectability to attitudes to animals which has underwritten thousands of years of exploitation and cruelty.

But simple observation inclines me to think that differences between human consciousness and that in other animals is, as with language, quantitative rather than qualitative. It may be a different, even unrecognisable kind of consciousness, but I'd argue that there must be something which allows these billions of different creatures simply to function on a daily basis. You might choose not to call that consciousness, but it might be that their variant on what we have doesn't oblige them to think (or, had they the ability, to write) about it at such interminable length.

I'm labouring this point about the similarities between ourselves and other animals, and I accept that what I've written about language and consciousness is probably absurdly reductionist. But I'm doing this for a good reason.

This is partly because another aspect of being human is the tendency to extrapolate from the perception of difference the idea of superiority, a widespread attitude that we don't just apply to different species, and which was merely compounded by Descartes. You can see this manifested in ideas like the Chain of Being, theological notions about our dominion over Nature, and even in how we think about evolution.

To simplify things massively, Darwin postulated the Theory of Evolution during a period of human history when science was beginning to supersede religion as the dominant intellectual and cultural way in which we seek to understand ourselves and our relationship to the universe. But as it did so it stole religion's eschatological clothes.

In its theological guise, present in many different religions from Christianity to the cults of the Aztec, eschatology is the idea of 'Last or Final Things', about how human destiny is inevitably and inexorably drawn towards an invariably cataclysmic final point in Time, which will be marked by the end of the world as we know it. In the nineteenth and twentieth centuries, this theological view of things inevitably getting worse coexisted with the scientific view that things were inevitably getting better. Both views are predicated on the belief that human existence, within the context of Time, necessarily involves some kind of linear progress. Because the way humans think is infinitely more complex, confused and frequently contradictory than either theologians or scientists tend to admit, there arose a common view that mingled and muddled both analyses. That's one reason why we're prone to scare ourselves serially witless with the idea that science will either lead us into or guide us out of the latest expectation of disaster, be it nuclear armageddon, global warming or the prospect of universal obesity.

The theological notion of progress towards annihilation is only a few thousand years old; the scientific (and thereafter cultural and social) idea of progress towards improvement (what we call 'Progress') is much, much more recent. The two interpretations of how we exist in Time, although cross-fertilising each other, are essentially dialectic opposites: the theological view predicts material disaster and oblivion, followed by things getting infinitely better in a solely nonmaterial dimension; the scientific view predicts that things will get better materially.[1]

Because Darwin's theories were clearly anti-theological, it followed that by and large they were seen as progressive in the scientific sense, and consequently in political and cultural ways too, both of themselves and in what they uncovered about the nature of our existence. Again confusing theology and science, this led to a widespread belief that the mechanism of evolution was there to improve things, was part of a linear process of constantly making things better, with ourselves as its perfect end point. Worse still, the first half of the twentieth century was deformed into monstrousness and mass murder by those who sought to accelerate this perception of evolution towards perfectibility through the pseudoscience of eugenics, a process that ended up in the gas chambers of the Nazis' Final Solution. But it also explains our tendency to talk about other creatures being 'further down the evolutionary scale' or the standard pictorial representation of the animal kingdom as a vertical tree, with us swaying in its uppermost branches. To be fair, most geneticists now use a visual model of a far more abstract tree, on its side, even if they also tend to have us at the

[1] There are an infinite number of cross-currents within these dynamics, as you'd expect, and it would be mistaken to assume that a religious view of Time means it's downhill all the way. In both Christianity and Islam (and, prospectively, Judaism too), the Incarnation of a Messiah or the appearance of Mohammed as God's Last Prophet mean that things have obviously got better. Then they get worse again before getting infinitely better after The End. Earlier, more animist theologies (which their successors obviously considered worse ones) often had different conceptions of Time. Some were circular, in which Time would either recur or partially recur to match the turn of the seasons, so Time could look either like a circle or an infinite spiralling helix. No one yet knows if the eschatologists (sacred or profane) or the animists are right.

right-hand end, with parallel taxa level with us, but with our genetic ancestors still trailing behind us. This is because we are unable to visualise this codification of our place in Time any other way, which itself is the result of our shortcomings in perception and the way our history and culture predispose us to think.

This popular view of evolution is, I believe, dangerously polluted by a host of other previous ideas, albeit ones which we have inevitably ascribed to it because of those limits to our perception. Most of us, I should imagine, think that in some either vague or palpable way we are 'better' than a slug, although a slug is absolutely perfectly adapted in every way imaginable to the requirements of being a slug. We think like that because we see evolution as a process towards Progress, rather than as a mechanism, the function of which is the continuous regulation of the system of life.

The idea of evolution has been summed up in the following rather unhelpfully opaque equation: evolution = natural selection + time. I think a better analogy is to think of evolution as like an air conditioning unit. If you imagine life on earth as a windowless room, survivability within that room is dependent on the air-conditioning, which modulates the temperature, up a bit now, down a bit then, in response to its thermostat, which in turn responds to the fluctuating temperature in the room. The unit just keeps on humming away in the corner forever, irrespective of who happens to be in the room at any particular time, and (because it's an air-conditioning unit) it's quite incapable of either judging the occupants or caring about their fate or even having any awareness of their existence.

It's important that we understand this, and that we also understand (to stick with this analogy) that each relatively tiny modulation which occurs in order to maintain regular room temperature is an expedient response to each changing circumstance in the varying temperature of the room, dealt with on a purely ad hoc basis. There is, in other words, no higher purpose, no overall plan, other than keeping the room habitable. Whether or not God installed the unit needn't bother us just yet.

We need to understand this in order to understand the nature of the world we inhabit and the system of life of which we're a part, but from which we are very definitely not *apart*. Within that system everything operates and is operated upon in the same way, shifting this way or that in order to deal, expediently and in an ad hoc way, with each fresh contingency. Each adaptation of form or behaviour, whether in the widest evolutionary terms or in how you decide where and when to cross the road, is operated on in this arbitrary and, I'm tempted to say, *purely accidental* fashion.

An almost perfect template for this exists within ourselves and everything else that's ever lived. Proselytising geneticists, keen to hit on a world-beating logo, talk up the simple, linear beauty of the double helix of the DNA molecule. I prefer to draw back a fraction and look at a gene sequence. To a geneticist's eye, this brachiated construct may well be clarity itself; to your average person, it's probably both baffling and largely irrelevant; but to my cartoonist's eye, a gene sequence looks exactly like a spatch-cock Heath Robinson contraption, with new genes bolted on any old how in order to keep the damn thing working to cope with whatever new fresh hell life and circumstances have thrown in its path.

I find this model of life as arbitrary, accidental, expedient and contingent not only makes sense, but also makes sense of everything else. I also find it rather comforting. It also places all of us in the same existentialist boat. We (and I'm including the whole of life in that sweeping pronoun) are all different, for different reasons, but we're also the same. The Archbishop of Canterbury, once we take the wider view, is practically indistinguishable from a slug or, for that matter, an HIV virus; meanwhile, the Archbishop of Canterbury and Richard Dawkins are so similar as to be, to all intents and purposes, identical.

Nonetheless, many of us, consciously or otherwise, persist in maintaining that there are absolute and qualitative differences between us and other animals. I recently attended a talk at London Zoo by the atheist geneticist Steve Jones in which he argued that we weren't actually animals at all, because we had language. (The same attitude, held for different reasons, was displayed in a TV programme a while ago when the atheist geneticist Richard Dawkins was thrown out of the home of an American Evangelist preacher, mid interview, because the preacher said that Dawkins was calling his children 'animals'.) Throughout the brief period of human history we can ever hope to know anything about, and the even briefer period we term, rather vaingloriously, as 'human civilisation', again and again we've come to the conclusion that that difference is delineated most clearly by our possession not just of language or consciousness, but also of a soul, a spiritual dimension to our being which links us with a higher and yet invisible and infinitely slippery thing we've termed God. We'll get back to him, her, it or them later, but in the meantime let's be content with satisfying ourselves that there is something else that divides us from our fellow species. Although different from language and consciousness, while also being inextricably linked up with each of them, this human quality not only marks a quantitative difference between us and other animals, but also explains why we keep pets and why we believe in God, why we worry so much more about the latter than the former, but also why both traits can be said, at a stretch, to define our humanity.

*

It's been calculated that a three-year-old human infant has a capacity for empathy several factors greater than an adult chimpanzee's. In other words, human infants can project their consciousness to seven degrees of separation. What that means is that they can imagine what it's like to be someone or, significantly, some*thing* else at up to seven removes from themselves. There are clearly sound evolutionary reasons for this, even though I'm as wary of accounting to evolution a proactive if unconscious role in determining our lives as I am of attributing any kind of conscious or unconscious determinism to God.

As we emerged, in fits and starts, into the hunting pack animals we basically are, it was to our advantage to utilise empathy, along with language which, as with consciousness, is maybe a consequence of empathy or its source. Just as a limpet has adapted to meet all the requirements necessary to function as a limpet, so we developed this capacity for imagination, the better to second-guess all the contingencies that might befall us, for purposes of survival, planning, organisation, communal living, social cohesion and all the other threads in the infinitely complex tapestry of being both alive and human.

Our species of hominid has been around for a comparatively short space of time, so there's every good reason to assume – unless you happen to be a Creationist – that the hominids we evolved from, as well as those that branched off from our common ancestors in other, ultimately less enduring directions, possessed this capacity too, to a lesser or maybe even a greater extent. The point, however, lies in the consequences of us developing empathy to the degree we have.

I've believed for a long time that as a species we are perfectly adapted to optimal living in the African plains hundreds of thousands of years ago, whispering to each other in our ur-language as we manoeuvre round whatever representative of Pleistocene megafauna our little pack of *Homo sapiens* are trying to entrap so we can eat it in order to survive, constantly second-guessing its next possible move by imagining what we'd do in its circumstances. In most other regards, however, we're hopeless.

Compared only to other animals, we're so stupid we can't fly without building incredibly complicated and disastrously filthy machines; we can't breathe underwater, or use echo location, or even maintain our body temperatures at comfortable or even survivable levels in most of the world's latitudes, without doing the same.[2] We are good at running and jumping, for a few years of our lives at any rate, and talking and laughing and having sex, but otherwise we have to go to school for years and years in order to be taught all the other things we now need simply in order to survive, because we're too stupid to work it out for ourselves. Even then, we're too stupid to work out the consequences of most of our actions. If you wanted to take the long view and get all Gaiaist about this, you might choose to see the whole history of human civilisation as one long, unwittingly scrawled suicide note for our entire species, with all its achievements and failures, its triumphs and tragedies and atrocities the accidental consequences of us growing brains overburdened with consciousness and empathy which,

[2] There's more to this than you might think. Our need to keep warm has led not only to our massive carbon footprint as a species, but also to deforestation in order to burn wood and thereafter build houses and hunting to extinction entire species of animal so we can wear their fur. Nor should we forget that the spark that ignited the Industrial Revolution, and all the social, political and environmental depredations that followed in its wake, was the desire to improve the manufacture of clothing from cotton. Add to that the political and military consequences of the cotton-growing monoculture of the slave-owning Southern states of America, or even today of the sweat shops of the so-called Third World, and the cost in human lives and misery of failing to live harmoniously as naked as nature intended becomes breathtaking.

purely as a by-product of that adaptation, allowed us to devise ways of reaching far beyond the defining circumstances which led to the initial adaptation. Sticking with Gaia, you might also choose to view the endless charivari of natural disasters we ceaselessly endure and which, so far, we've survived, as Gaia doing her very best to shrug us off, like a nasty cold.

But let's not get too judgemental quite yet. Nor should we indulge too deeply in ideas of super-consciousnesses, however well intentioned or metaphorical their invocation. Instead, let's stay with empathy.

As an innate, hard-wired evolutionary survival tool, empathy allows human beings to project their own individual consciousness in all directions, which we do constantly and incontinently because we can't do anything else. It allows us to love other human beings, and to hate them, but more importantly to imagine what it's like for them to be loved or hated, and thereafter what it's like for them to love or hate us. From our capacity to imagine what it's like to be someone else also spring pity, compassion, generosity, envy, jealousy, covetousness, revenge, hope and remorse. I'd suggest it's also what moulds the intensity of almost all of our other human emotions. It also made it possible for us to view the world around us, project ourselves into it and beyond the horizon and then report back so we could reflect on the position and condition we found ourselves in and act accordingly. This isn't either a spiritual or physical extension of ourselves beyond ourselves, but the result of our capacity for imagination; it's not anything 'paranormal' like thought transference or telepathy, although that's what it actually is, but it is innate and of ourselves. Just like the Bishop of Southwark, it's *what we do*, because we're human.

A further consequence of this is the way it allows us to attempt to make sense of our world by using methods to control it, both individually and collectively. For this we can thank our enhanced empathetic capacity to build imaginatively on memories of the past and thus imagine possible futures

We sought to control the world in other ways, consequent upon our capacity for language and our opposable thumbs and forefingers. We sought to control the experiences of our lives by retelling them, filtering them through our individual consciousness and thus recreating them; and by talking about ourselves, language found its true human métier, not simply as a medium of instruction, but through high and low gossip, the real songlines with which we mapped the world around us. We filtered and sought to control the world in other ways too, by recreating it in paintings daubed on cave walls, and we've continued to do so ever since, either representationally or imaginatively, in every genre all the way up to political cartoons. Hence, in a nutshell, art and literature, and also music, through which we recreate and echo the rhythms of our world and our lives.

Thereafter we operated on a more interventionist level: we grabbed each passing contingency, and along the way developed agriculture, which led to permanent settlements, notions of property, wars to dispute that property, kings to fight those wars, capitalism to fund the kings, different politics to counter the capitalism, and on it goes.[3] And another aspect of the desire for control is the urge to understand: hence inquiry, philosophy, science, politics and economics and also, of course, religion. I believe that these are all accidental by-products of our capacity for empathy, but most importantly, all have their source within us as human beings and nowhere else.

[3] Capitalism, of course, is based entirely on our ability imaginatively to second-guess the future, and predicated exclusively on a faith in the efficacy of prophesy, just like Nostradamus or the Book of Revelation.

So, thanks to empathy we project our individual consciousness into everything around us which then, like a million million mirrors, bounces back the projection and reflects us back to ourselves. But the mirrors don't just reflect: in our perception of them, we imagine they absorb something of us too. That's why, probably uniquely of all the animal species that have ever lived, we keep pets.[4] It's because we imbue them with our own qualities which then reflect back on us and to our own advantage, and thus make us feel better. After all, the appearance of requited or recip-

[4] I say probably, because there are a few instances of different species co-habiting in ways which go beyond the usual imperatives of eating or being eaten, or engaging in some kind of mutually advantageous symbiosis. One example of this happened in the Tower of London Menagerie, a few centuries after Henry III's polar bear lived there. It was the practice of the Tower authorities to let the public in half-price to see the lions and tigers if they brought with them a puppy or kitten to throw into the lions' den. This is now called behavioural enrichment. However, in the late seventeenth century one such unfortunate whelp was not instantly torn to pieces and eaten by the lions, but instead lived on in their pit to a ripe old age. One explanation for this phenomenon, expressed at the time, was that one of the lionesses had recently lost a cub, and so transferred her maternal instincts onto the dog. Although this is another frequently stated explanation for why we, as humans, keep pets, I think it's too reductionist: while I'm not denying the presence of empathy in other animals, the point I'm trying to make is its exceptional level in human beings. Nor am I too bothered about where it came from or why, suffice it to say that a trait which prevents male humans, by and large, from killing their own children or other people's, unlike many other male animals, is probably an evolutionary advantage. Incidentally, if you're shocked by the Tower Menagerie's admissions policy, for centuries the English were notorious throughout Europe for their cruelty to animals, and citizens of the Inquisitors' Spain or the Kingdom of the Two Sicilies would blanch with horror when they heard about our predilection for bull- and bear-baiting, or how the gentry, in their Palladian mansions overlooking forcibly enclosed parkland freshly landscaped by Capability Brown, would often have a pond by the terrace, filled with pike, into which they'd toss live chickens after dinner.

rocated love, however inarticulate, is just as capable as the real thing of releasing all those lovely endorphins, the hormones our bodies release to make us feel good. And it's not only pets. It's toys, teddy bears, dolls, knick-knacks and gee gaws, a favourite chair or a precious souvenir, even bits of soggy old blanket we hug and suck to destruction for comfort. We imbue all of them with levels of importance to us they hardly merit objectively, and although this is, in many ways, motivated by the same things which draw a dog to its bone, its intensity and scope is, albeit quantitatively, uniquely human.

For precisely the same reason, and in exactly the same way, the same goes for God too.

What? Calling God a comfort blanket is a common insult hurled by secularists at the religious in order to mock their implied childishness. But God as invisible sky pet? Well, why not? It's just as convincing a paradigm as God the imaginary friend, and both more convincing and more charming than the notion that God is actually real.

*

Not that I'm saying that God doesn't exist. In fact he, she, it or they clearly do exist, but in a very particular way, which is again concomitant on our capacity for empathy. A few years ago some child psychologists in America showed a group of young children some Bugs Bunny cartoons, and thereafter asked the children whether or not they thought that Bugs was really alive. All the children answered that they thought that he was, although obviously not in the same way as they themselves were alive. That sums it up rather neatly, and not because of the supposed or assumed naivety or gullibility of the children. In seeking to explain and control the world around us we also, as I've said, have this capacity to extend our consciousness over the horizon to report back to us, and we do this by using our imaginations. All of us spend our entire lives imagining things which aren't there, with a clarity and palpability which parallels our perception of what is palpably and observably in front of our eyes. If we didn't do this, we wouldn't be human, and if we couldn't we'd be extinct. Among other things we imagine which aren't there are things in the future, things in the past, things in the minds and motivations of other people, other animals, even inanimate objects. Jane Austen imagined Mr Darcy, and therefore, on paper or on screen, and in our minds, Mr Darcy exists, even though he's not real.

Mike Maltese, one of the scriptwriters at the Warner Brothers' animation unit, used to tell a story about a party he once went to in Hollywood where his hostess asked him what he did, and he replied that he wrote jokes for Bugs Bunny. With a giggle of surprise and disbelief, she replied 'Don't be silly! Bugs Bunny doesn't need a joke writer! He's already funny!' By the same token an eighteenth century bishop confided to a friend, after he'd finished reading Jonathan Swift's *Gulliver's Travels*, that he didn't believe a single word of it. Along with the children being monitored by those psychologists, it's tempting to dismiss both the Hollywood hostess and the bishop as gullible and stupid, but just because I happen to know that Bugs' observably real existence consists solely of a series of drawings filmed singly and in sequence so that they'll give the illusion of movement and a false kind of life when projected at sufficient speed against a screen on beams of light, that doesn't mean that he's not real in all sorts of different ways, and therefore 'alive' in other ways too, including the infinitely long half-life he lives in my imagination.

As with Bugs Bunny, so with Mr Darcy. And so with God. Indeed, in his various guises Yahweh is one of the most fascinating characters in the whole of literature. Proscriptive, prescriptive, vengeful, violent, loving, contradictory, cruel, forgiving, irrational, he's a perfect mirror held up to ourselves, and just as flawed as we are, his supposed control of human affairs displaying either incredible incompetence or breathtaking callousness. These are shortcomings we can recognise in ourselves and in everyone around us.

For this and many other reasons, as far as I'm concerned, of all the creations of human culture, religion is absolutely the least mysterious. True, to maintain its potent grip on the human imagination from whence it arose, religion perpetually swathes itself in mystery, whether it's the nature of the Trinity, transubstantiation, the unknowability and imperceptibility of God or the sound of one hand clapping. (For the record, the sound of one hand clapping is almost identical to the sound of two fists clenching. Try it yourself.) Then again, we all love a good mystery, whether it's Miss Marple or the Hypostatic Union, and this is probably as an attentuated by-product of an early adaptation in brain patterns to help us solve all the tiny problems life throws at us on a daily basis. Nevertheless, none of these mysteries is actually all that mysterious, unless you want them to be. Otherwise, it's not only obvious why religion exists, but also how it operates and why people believe in it. Anthropologically, sociologically, culturally, psychologically, biologically and even theologically, religion is really a bit of a no-brainer. I even feel slightly embarrassed in spelling it out: how religion is merely an ontological stopgap, a makeweight for our own shortcomings in perception which initially took root because we're predisposed to project ourselves beyond our individuality to help us position ourselves to our satisfaction and comfort in the world around us in order to function properly.

But religion is more than that too, and more than simply a repository for us to extend ourselves into something we perceive as larger and more awesome and important than ourselves, although that's one of the ways it's maintained its potency and attraction. But remember that we're social animals; it's to our advantage to respond positively to collectivist imperatives beyond our individual selves.

That said, although they operate in parallel and in unison, consciousness and empathy are also in constant conflict. All we can possibly hope truly, or even adequately, to know is in and of our individual selves. Everything else beyond that individual, personal sense of self is guesswork, albeit usually well founded. We've evolved in ways that allow us to do that, but it's interesting to observe how ill at ease we are as a species with our brains, our minds and the instincts with which we've been equipped.

You could take that constant dilemma between how our consciousness and our capacity for empathy make us behave as something else which defines us as human. We hate loneliness, but guard our privacy and value moments of solitude; but long term solitary confinement is a particularly exquisite punishment, one that many of us might think is a fate worse than death. Nonetheless, as we all know, and as the French existentialist atheist Jean-Paul Sartre told us sixty years ago, Hell Is Other People. To upend and paraphrase the eroticist and Anglican divine John Donne, each man is an island, but also part of a larger archipelago, oscillating between federation and war.

As I've already observed, unlike limpets (we assume), we spend a ridiculous amount of time thinking about how and why we think (including writing a book like this). And yet as a species we also spend an enormous amount of time and effort seeking ways to escape from the default setting of our brains. Just as no human society has existed without doing something like keeping pets or observing religious rituals, there's also no human society I can think of that hasn't sought out some kind of catalyst towards transcendence. By that I mean some external method of making you feel different from the way you would otherwise, whether that's alcohol, cigarettes, drugs, obsessive exercise, Benylin cough mixture with vodka chasers, rhythmical drumming, chanting, meditation or generally abusing our bodies in order to change our minds. If you wanted to, I suppose you could argue that this is the best evidence there is for the kind of dualism Descartes described: the body merely provides the means of locomotion for the brain, which in turn is the seat of the soul or mind, so it follows that you whack the body with whatever psychotropic means there is to hand to transform the mind, irrespective of what damage is wrought on the body. I'm told that you experience amazing visions if you don't eat for three weeks, which is probably just as much fun as you'll get from a bottle of whisky or a syringe full of smack.[5] And it's significant that many of these essays in mind-altering behaviour take place within a religious context.

*

[5] This universal trait towards psychotropic transcendence is just another, although maybe regrettable, manifestation of our humanness, which is more bad news for all those well-intentioned people who'd like us to stop. Whenever my children would come home from school from yet another drugs- or drink-awareness lecture, I'd always ask them if the lecturer had pointed out that people gobble Ecstasy because it's fun, irrespective of the inherent dangers involved. Of course they'd done nothing of the kind, and instead just tried to terrify the children into good behaviour, implying that all substance abuse would inevitably lead to instant death. This is, if you'll forgive me for saying so, an incredibly stupid tactic, because it patently isn't true, and while sawing your own head off might indeed lead to the most amazing high ever, it's pretty obvious why most people choose not to seek their thrills in that particular way.

I'm not making yet another cheap crack at religion by pointing out the role of peyote in the devotional habits of many Native Americans, or of the sacramental centrality of magic mushrooms to certain shamanistic practices, or the part played by dizzying quantities of booze in propitiating the Greek god Dionysus, and how you can detect a more moderate echo of that in the metaphorical role played by wine in the Christian recreation of Christ's Last Supper. What these mood- or mind-altering substances do is, without question, extraordinary, and like many other extraordinary, or often quite ordinary, aspects of our existence and experience, the way we use them long ago started to be treated as something special, then something to be venerated, and then as sacred.

This is something else we're predisposed to do because we're human. Because we're able to imagine what it might be like not to be confined within the narrowness of everyday human existence, we've aspired to and often succeeded in escaping it. Among the things outside what you might call normal human experience is madness, and we've succeeded very well in discovering and devising all sorts of different ways of driving ourselves temporarily mad, and we enjoy doing it too. We're not alone in this. It's well documented that many other animals actively seek out their own psychotropic catalysts, one example being the fruit bats who prefer to eat rotting and therefore fermenting fruit, because its alcohol content gets them pissed.

Another human quality present in animals is play, or pretending to do something you're not really doing. But once more we've developed this to extraordinary levels, and been duly amazed by what we've done. If you think about it (which we did), pretending to be someone else is truly weird, as well as hazardous, and so we venerated it and then made it sacred: remember that Greek drama, the first theatre we really know about, was performed as part of a religious rite during the annual Athenian feast of Dionysus. And we continue to venerate actors, although in different if equally respectful ways, propitiating them with levels of money, attention and affection that they hardly seem to deserve.

But our empathy also compels us to imbue the mundane with extraordinary qualities, and in their turn they, too, have been treated as special, then venerated, then as sacred. This includes something as basic and mundane as eating which is also, of course, central to our survival.

One explanation I've already suggested for the adaptation which equipped us with our levels of empathy, and possibly language too, is that it enabled us to hunt more efficiently, allowing us constantly to second-guess the next possible actions of our prey. But a consequence, or more correctly an accidental by-product, of that adaptation has been our ability to imagine what it's like to be that animal, to inhabit its mind and imagine its terror and fear, and the sadness and horror of it being killed and then eaten. I doubt that many other animals do this in the way we can, to the point where many of us defy our omnivores' guts and the imperatives of our nutritional needs by eschewing the eating of meat because we think it's cruel.

An alternative way of coping with this horrific dilemma is to honour your prey in various different ways. Many hunter-gatherers venerate the creatures they kill; in many other human societies throughout history that veneration has slowly accreted into sacredness, sometimes ending with deification, but more commonly with elaborate rituals of sacrifice.

The shores of the Mediterranean are littered with the remains of altars surrounded by the bones of the animals slaughtered on them. Different gods demanded different creatures, one god preferring fish, another having a fondness for pigs while a third demanded the beheading of a horse, and so on. It's tempting, now, to see in this a wanton cruelty, the further exploitation of other species to appease our delusions. But the whole point of sacrifice is that it is deeply respectful, and entails giving away something you need or want precisely because you value it highly.[6] The respect, in the first instance, is aimed towards the creature due for sacrifice, because we, as humans, not only value the animal, but also imagine we know what it's like to be that animal, what it will be like for it to be dead, how it will feel about that and how we will too. I strongly suspect that the sacrifices came long before the gods that latterly lent them some kind of justification once we'd wised up to how this fresh cruelty didn't, after all, exonerate us from all the previous acts of cruelty.

This applies especially to human sacrifice. Our instinct, as social animals, is collectivist, which makes us value each other and each other's life. One of the more extraordinary things humans can do is kill each other, which is why it remains a universal taboo, even though humans do it constantly, although almost only in the specific context of more severe individual or collective trauma. But as expending a human life is absolutely the worst thing you can do to someone else, it's also to be valued the greatest, and thereafter could be seen as absolutely the most respectful thing imaginable if confronted with other contingencies you

[6] There are, as you'd expect, infinite variations on this, including sacrificing things not because you value them, but because your enemies do, even if it means that you, too, end up losing out. It's been suggested that the French proclivity for eating horses is an example of this. Horses are not obvious food in usual circumstances, because they fulfil other, more useful functions, and are therefore too valuable an economic resource to waste by serving up at table. However, following the French Revolution, eating the horses of the aristocracy was a revolutionary act, displaying a zealous contempt for both the oppressor and his property.

seek to control, like the seasons or the weather. Again, it's likely that the idea of the sacredness of the act predated the gods it was later believed it propitiated.

The potency of the idea of sacrifice is ubiquitous. Before the Iraq War, the Christian and then prime minister Tony Blair made a speech in which he referred, bizarrely and rather chillingly, to the blood debt we owed the Americans for the Second World War (although he failed to mention the far greater blood debt we must, therefore, owe the Russians). After the Restoration of Charles II, one of the few surviving regicides who'd signed Charles I's death warrant to escape execution was the wit, libertine, Leveller, extreme republican and probable atheist Harry Marten, who Cromwell called 'an ugly rogue and a whoremonger' when he dissolved the Rump Parliament in 1653. One of the arguments that saved Marten's life (he was sentenced, instead, to life imprisonment) was that the execution of the regicides was itself a form of sacrifice, to expiate the collective sin of killing the King and shedding his sacred blood, and that Marten was such a notorious rogue that he was an unworthy offering. (See Appendix B.)

And, as we know, the idea of sacrifice extends to the most valuable thing we can ever know, which is our individual selves. Self-sacrifice is another of those human activities which make us feel good, about ourselves and other people. That's why, at one level, we give to charity; but also why we respond positively to totally unreasonable injunctions like Jesus Christ's dictum that the greatest love is to give up your life for your friends; it's what inspired, though with different consequences, the terminal actions of both Sydney Carton and Mohammed Ata, or the antepenultimate actions of Christ himself. These, in turn, inspire us, although again in different ways depending on your point of view.

*

At whatever stage religion as we now understand it emerged, it's clear that it's been an engine for social cohesion as well as a mechanism for social control, a conduit for the codification of protocols to ensure smoother collective cohabitation as well as a blunt instrument for imposing modes of behaviour. The structures of religion have provided countless templates for the ritualisation of human interaction with our environment in all its seen and unseen manifestations, as well as the ritualisation of our responses to and behaviour in the presence of the greatest and potentially most mysterious events in everyone's lifetime: reproduction and death.

Because we can imagine the future, and because the deaths of other people provide a constant leit motif to our own lives, we can imagine our own deaths with probably greater clarity than any other animal. Again, this is a consequence of our heightened senses of empathy and consciousness. It's unknown, or at least unclear, at what point in our evolution as a species we developed our capacity for grief, and thus began to build up our complex rituals surrounding it, although there is evidence that Neanderthals (our genetic cousins, not forebears, with whom we coexisted for thousands of years) buried their dead along with grave goods, suggesting some kind of belief in a possible afterlife. Then again, elephants and hippopotamuses have been observed lingering round the remains of dead members of their herds, displaying signs of distress which are so much like grief that there's no real point in calling it anything else. Likewise, we don't know when we first made a conscious casual connection between sex and birth, or for that matter if gerbils recognise it as clearly as we do. Nonetheless, it's no surprise that religion, as a societal phenomenon, should place such great emphasis on both reproduction and death. Nor is it that surprising that some religions, being extensions of our

individual bewilderment at the actual which transforms it
into the amazing and the sacredly special, should proscribe
sex and deny death, while other religions enthusiastically
and proatively embrace both. Religions do this for the same
reason that we make jokes about the same things, this being
simply another mechanism, probably hard wired into us as
an evolutionary survival tool, to stop us all going mad with
existentialist terror and to help us make another stab at
controlling the uncontrollable.[7]

I could go on and on cataloguing the different ways in
which religion has provided a method for responding to the
realities of human existence and experience, but all that
really needs to be said is that each one, with its basis in
human reactions to human conditions, suggests that
religion's origins lie firmly and exclusively within ourselves.
In other words, religion is just another human activity. If you
like, you could even describe it (as the unfriendly vicar at the

[7] I've left out the third part of the Trinity of the Great Mysteries of Life,
which is, of course, shit. Although I'm not aware of many or indeed
any religions which venerate this foul stuff that pours out of our bodies
on at least a daily basis, its credentials for being treated as sacred are
impeccable. It is, after all, relatively sophisticated of us consciously to
recognise the connection between eating and shitting, given our
tendency to make the wrong connections with regard to so many other
things in our lives and in our world. It's worth mentioning that, along
with sex and death (frequently attenuated into the misfortunes of
others), we laugh at shit probably more than at anything else, although
usually in a relatively crude way. That said, I've often thought that if
there can be said to be an ur-humour, an elemental and universal
something that we all find funny, then it could be typified thus:
PHWSSST! That is, as a raspberry, the noise the shit makes as it issues
from our bodies, and which in my admittedly limited experience is
guaranteed to make babies and young children roll about shrieking
with laughter, even if anyone older in the room usually maintains an
air of aloof, stony-faced maturity. Given that religion and laughter are
two sides of the same coin, and not necessarily in the way you might
assume, it seems rather strange (while simultaneously being pretty

party tried to), as a dimension of our humanity, even up to
the point where it defines that humanity. In this regard,
religion isn't a good thing or a bad thing: it's just a thing, as
open to or immune from criticism as anything else we choose
to engage in to fill the empty days, whether it's trainspotting
or gene-splicing or journalism. But everything about it its
elites, its mysteries, its mysteriousness, its tendencies to tolerance or intolerance, its loves, its hates, its rituals, its hegemonic
urges, its rules, its dogmas, its illogicalities, its ridiculousness,
its beauty and its certainty, have clear parallels in most other
human activities. There is, however, neither evidence of nor
even a particular requirement for any external agency to be
involved.

Actually, I'd be slightly more impressed by religion if it
was less patently mundane and more obviously super-
natural: if, for example, Osama Bin Laden had collapsed the
twin towers of the World Trade Center on 11 September
2001 with the breath exhaled from his nostrils, rather than

obvious) why religion has steered well clear of shit, given some of the
other extraordinary byways of human behaviour that religion has
meandered down over the centuries. Nonetheless, I can only think of
one specificially shit-related religious moment, when the Emperor
Vespasian, dying of dysentery, commented as he fell into the arms of
one of his attendants after a valedictory and final purgation, 'Vae puto
deus fio!' ['Oh dear! I think I'm becoming a god!']. Another thought,
concerning the length of lower gut surgically removed from Pope John
Paul II after his attempted assassination on 13 May 1981, is just me
being gratuitously offensive. Still, with a little bit of forethought
someone could have popped the slithery thing into a reliquary against
the happy day of John Paul's canonisation, after which one would
fervently hope that, each year on his saint's day, it would expel a
miraculous stool which, once rubbed into the affected body parts of the
supplicant sick, could be expected to effect an instantaneous cure.
Irrelevantly but alluringly, we shouldn't here forget the vaguely
appropriate old joke from James Joyce's Ulysses about how Christ
turned the water into wine, and how thereafter the wedding guests
turned the wine back into water.

killing 3,000 people he'd never met by getting some murderously muddle-headed young men to steal aircraft designed by cleverer men than them in order to kill themselves and many, many others by flying into buildings designed and built by other clever men. Likewise, if, during his annual Urbi et Orbi address from the balcony of St Peter's, the Pope suddenly grew to 10,000 times his original size and squirted mighty jets of milk, honey and amniotic fluid from his fingertips, I might (but only might) be inclined to pay more attention to his opinions on what women should do with their bodies. Even the afore-mentioned Dr Rowan Williams, currently the Archbishop of Canterbury, might grab my attention more effectively if, when he started intoning in that pained baritone of his, he did so while scurrying across the ceiling like a gecko.

Of course, I understand quite clearly that faith should not and cannot depend simply on vulgar spectacle.

I understand that only too well.

*

However, while I find religion easily understandable, and both its origins and the way it operates explicable in relatively simple terms, I don't 'get' it. I don't 'get' it in the same way that I don't 'get' P. G. Wodehouse[8] or Association Football[9]. And when I say I don't get it, what I really mean

[8] This admission is akin to blasphemy among certain Englishmen of a particular class, irrespective of their ethnicity or chosen nationality. These include Salman Rushdie, author of The Satanic Verses, Francis Wheen, author of How Mumbo-jumbo Conquered the World: A Short History of Modern Delusions and Christopher Hitchens, author of God Is Not Great.
[9] By the way, professional football and religion provide neat analogies for each other. Each probably had its origins in providing a structure to reinforce communal solidarity while having a bit of fun at the same time, which built up, then depended on and finally exploited the

is that I can't see the attraction. This goes beyond my 'lack of faith' or failure to be persuaded by religion's various explanations of all sorts of different things. Obviously, given what I've already written, I find alternative explanations far more compelling and, for that matter, comforting, but I also concede that I find most things to do with religion and, indeed, the religiously minded, deeply irritating. To give them their due, they'd probably feel the same about me if they thought about it. Still, here are some of the things I don't 'get' about religion.

For a start, I simply cannot see why I should worship my creator. That's not to say that I don't understand why it should be expected of me, but that's something else entirely, which I'll address later. In the meantime, I acknowledge that if I accept that I had a personal creator at all, beyond my parents and their parents and so on, a certain amount of respect or simple gratitude might be in order, but that's quite different from worship. This may be a rather puerile observation (though I also see no reason why we should be quite so dismissive of the opinions of little boys compared to anyone else), but the need for worship doesn't really reflect too well on God. Ignoring for a moment the thousands of years of human speculation about the nature of God, whether he, she, it or they is merely the Prime

enthusiasm and consequent unquestioning loyalty of a large number of supporters who experience all sorts of heightened emotions, up to and including mindless violence, spectating an event which is, of itself, relatively boring. Then it all went wrong, corrupted by money and power. Modern professional football, in the Premier League at least, now rivals the court of the Borgia Pope in the depths of its venality, avarice, decadence and debauchery. Professional football is also one of the few remaining bulwarks of rampant homophobia, despite the fact that it, along with the Catholic Church or silly, sexually repressed young men with bad beards jumping through barbed-wire hoops in secret training facilities on the Pakistan/Afghan border, is among the campest things you're ever likely to see.

Mover or pays particular daily care over all our lives, I feel distinctly uneasy about a being, whatever its unknowable nature, requiring not only my belief in its existence, like Tinkerbell in J. M.Barrie's *Peter Pan*, but my unquestioning devotion as well. Whatever form this being may or may not take, whether it be some inchoate life force buzzing through the universe or an old man with a white beard up in the sky, I just don't know why God should expect me specifically to demean, belittle and humiliate myself in those ways that are inevitably a part of worshipping anything. Unless, that is, God is actually some kind of inter-dimensional faith para-site, a bit like an enormous tape worm, who's just feeding on us all. (By the same token, I don't get why God should have created the Universe in the first place, except in order to create beings to worship him, her, it or them, which seems to me to be a pretty squalid, if all too human, reason to do anything. Even so, the Catholic Catechism includes the lines 'Why did God make me? God made me to know him, love him and serve him in this world and be happy ever after with him in the next'.[10])

Of course, those people who believe in and worship God will answer that because God is Love, it's only proper – maybe even simply polite – to repay that love, although I still don't get it. Another stock answer is that I shouldn't question these things because I cannot ever hope to know the mind of God. But that's just a cop-out and no answer at all. You could fill a million libraries for a million years with encyclopaedias a million volumes long listing things that I can never hope to understand or even comprehend. They include the precise (if unreliable) workings of the machine I'm writing this book on, and also other things practically no one understands at all, like string theory. Indeed, the German physicist Werner Heisenberg said that the structure of the atom, which is the

---

[10] I need to thank the great cartoonist Posy Simmonds for this insight.

building block of everything, was almost literally incomprehensible to the human mind. But I'm not going to start praying to an atom either.

I admit that this says more about the shortcomings of my mind than it says about either God or atoms, but these are shortcomings that affect all of us. Nor, clearly, should I leap to universal conclusions because of my own ignorance. But that, of course, is exactly what human beings have always done, and in many ways God is the simplest conclusion we could possibly have leapt to, and the most simplistic as well. That's another reason I don't and can't buy it, given the mind-numbing complexity of everything else around me.

I also don't get it when believers accuse non-believers of arrogance when they deny the existence of God. It seems to me the height of arrogance to assume that something or someone that created the whole universe should be in the slightest bit interested in all those funny little over-evolved monkeys scampering around on a planet far from the centre of the cosmos, and given the evidence of human misery and catastrophe, he, she, it or they clearly aren't that bothered anyway. Certain hope of life after death also strikes me as being unbelievably arrogant, particularly as it's often doctrinally exclusive, no matter how much you might want to believe in a heaven that's got room for your pussy cat or even your friends who disagree with you.

But once more the answer will come back that God's ways are unknowable to me, and round we go again till your head starts to hurt, and the temptation to paraphrase Wittgenstein becomes overpowering: that of which we cannot think, perhaps we should stop thinking about altogether.

At the moment that doesn't appear to be an option even though, as I've just demonstrated, the argument between the religious and the non-religious can never be more than a bad-tempered slanging match, because both sides are arguing from different and incompatible premises.

*

Not that that stops scientifically minded secularists from fostering a metaphysics of their own. In answer to the rather fatuous accusation that denial of God denies us both a sense of meaning and a sense of awe (we only need the first because we think we do; we experience the second about all sorts of things apart from God), they often cite the numinous[11] beauty of the double helix of the DNA molecule or the view of the universe from the Hubble Space Telescope. Interestingly, as with God, both these things are invisible to the naked eye, and you can only see them thanks to the intercessionary skills of a highly trained caste of specialists: in other words, a priesthood.

There are other scientific metaphysics. In my earlier description of the mechanics of evolution, I maybe failed to emphasise the central role played by time. Evolution takes place imperceptibly slowly, in our perception at least, and thus to all intents and purposes takes on the attributes of God as described by the Christian poet, revolutionary and satirist John Milton in *Paradise Lost*: unperceived but understood.

There are other priesthoods too, which share all the attributes of religious priesthoods. We all recognise the different elites who use their elite status to seek to dictate the ways we should live our lives, and who conduct their affairs in identical ways. They all require lengthy initiations into arcane knowledge, involve secret languages and claim a greater or deeper knowledge which they then say we should all unquestioningly accept. In large parts of the Western world the dominant priesthoods at the moment are

[11] I had to look this word up when I first came across it in the Acknowledgements section of Christopher Hitchens' *God Is Not Great*. It means 'pertaining to a divinity' or 'suffused with a feeling of divinity'. He used it to describe the novels of Ian McEwan, the book's dedicatee, so maybe Hitchens should have looked it up too.

legal and medical. Leaving the lawyers to themselves for the moment, the medical priesthood can be seen as an exact parallel to the religious, although offering potentially infinitely prolonged life instead of never-ending life after death, wrought through what most of the laity can only perceive as miracles. There's also an assumption to infalli-bility, despite serial errors and failures. More than that, under the priesthood of the doctors a new and dangerous kind of theology has developed, which they've encouraged, or at least done nothing to forestall. Perhaps inevitably, scientific and medical analyses of the vagaries of human existence have led to a widespread belief – or, if you prefer, faith – that every negative aspect of that existence has the potential to be cured. Whether it's infertility or just a general sense of vague unhappiness, all can now be 'cured' to a greater or lesser degree. This in turn has, I believe, turned things on their head, and led to a new and universal doctrine: because so many negative parts of our life can be diagnosed, once more we've leapt to yet another conclusion and come to believe that *every* part of our lives can be diagnosed. Thus all aspects of our existence become patho-logical and life itself is seen as just another chronic medical condition. And the doctors keep upping the ante, although they also keep changing their minds to maintain us in a constant state of mystification. So one week we're meant to eat this, the next that; meanwhile, we're too thin, or too fat; and we're always, always doing this, that or the other thing wrong. And, of course, all this is *our* fault. Once upon a time we were born into original sin. These days it seems we're born into original illness instead.

Anyway, in addition to the charge of arrogance laid against the godless by the godly, there's the additional charge of immorality, or more precisely amorality. Although I clearly understand why this is said – it's intended to be an insult, and it's also staking an exclusive claim to something we all possess to a lesser or greater degree – I find this gambit offensive and irritating in equal measure. And it's also something else I don't 'get', probably because I'm instantly suspicious whenever anyone starts talking about morality, a bit like the lion-owning Hermann Goering reaching for his revolver whenever he heard the word 'culture'. This is because those who talk about it the most usually practise it the least, and not solely because of the innate hypocrisies of human frailty. (It's also because the only one of the seven deadly sins most religious moralists ever seem that bothered about is lust, and although they sometimes have a crack at avarice, when was the last time you heard a bishop, a cardinal, an imam or a rabbi denouncing sloth?)

Morality is another of those things which humans have developed for sound reasons which they then imbue with an external existence beyond themselves. As far as I'm concerned, morality fits perfectly with the evolutionary template I outlined above, adapting in changing circumstances, and it's based entirely in us, as a species, attempting to establish a set of contingent protocols to accommodate human cohabitation. As such, it's something else which has its origins solely within us and the way we interact with each other.

And, once more, I'd argue that the germ of morality is to be found in our capacity for empathy. If you think of the people in the world around you as inhabiting a series of concentric circles rippling out from you at the centre, then the further you extend your sense of empathy, by considering the effect of your actions on other people (and, indeed, things) and determining those actions accordingly, the less harm you'll do and the greater will be your 'morality'.

I think it really is as simple as that. I also think that that recognition (articulated by Jesus Christ among others) is at the core of all human ideas about 'good' and 'evil'. You can

find this idea expressed perfectly in the Christian allegorist
and satirist Dante Alighieri's vision of hell in his *Inferno*.
Hell, too, is a series of concentric circles, but with an added,
third dimension, to give it the appearance of an inverted
cone. The circles highest and widest contain the mildest
sinners; as they get narrower and deeper, the sinfulness of
their occupants is greater, until you reach the frozen ninth
circle, the smallest and deepest with the tightest circum-
ference, containing the worst sinners of all. In Dante's view,
this was reserved for the traitors against their lords or
benefactors, and contained Brutus, Cassius, Judas Iscariot and
Satan himself, the incarnation of evil, his three heads devour-
ing the other inmates for all eternity. The intensity of its
claustrophobic hellishness lies as much, for us social animals,
in the loneliness and isolation of its unhappy inhabitants as in
the torments of cold and mastication they suffer.

That said, I doubt 'evil' objectively exists, except in the
perception of other people, and we return to that contradiction we all display between purely personal consciousness
and the collectivist feelings our capacity for empathy
compels us to experience. Although all of us constantly do
'bad' things, we only do them in the first place because we
think they're good. Even a clear perception of the 'badness'
of any action doesn't invalidate this, it's just that the way it
makes us feel good outweighs all other considerations. Each
of our lives is made up of an infinite series of tiny judgement
calls, acting exactly like the process of evolution in
modulating our behaviour as we navigate our way through
life (and don't forget that the mechanism of evolution
appears to be extraordinarily wasteful and has given rise to
vast numbers of dead ends or, if you find the loaded
language of judgement more comfortable or comprehen-
sible, 'mistakes'), and this applies in the case of morality as
much as anywhere else. The point is, the way we feel about

our actions affecting other people is hard-wired into us, and the extent of our numbness to those feelings is what defines whether our actions, and therefore we ourselves, are 'good' or 'evil'. The idea of numbness or physical insensitivity to the feelings or sufferings of other people is epitomised in the derivation of the word 'callousness', from the phenomenon of hard and insensitive human skin.

The Nazis, for instance, considered themselves to be good people. Worse than that, they worked actively to make life for the German people better, and those people themselves perfect, which is obviously as good as you can possibly get. They were not, by their own lights, actively immoral, and in practice they were utterly merciless towards people who they thought were. But not only was the range of their empathy limited solely to those their perverted science deemed to be racially pure Germans, they denied the humanity of everyone else outside this circle. The Italian Jewish scientist and writer Primo Levi, describing his experiences in Auschwitz, wrote of how one of his Nazi interrogators looked at him like something in an aquarium, something no longer human.

This deliberate constraint or denial of simple human empathy is what made the Nazis uniquely evil, and the word is used precisely. In the quality of their evil, they clearly outstripped the possibly greater, quantitative evil of Stalin or Mao or the Khmer Rouge, because the murders committed by Stalin and his imitators were largely committed expeditiously, to remove their political enemies, whether former allies or more general enemies of their political programmes, who even in their enmity still per-sisted in maintaining their value as human, however much they were individually dehumanised to make their slaughter more bearable for their killers. But the Nazis saw their victims merely as inconvenient things, which just had to be got rid of because they were in the way.

This is as vilely and repulsively anti-human as you can get, but it goes without saying that Hitler and Stalin and the rest of them naturally assumed that they were making things better, and probably even saw some morality in their actions, as they set about being as immoral as it's conceivable to be. Without intending to offend those unhappy humans whose limited capacity for empathy seriously impairs their ability to function in human society, you could call this kind of psychotic selfishness Moral Autism.[12]

In explaining these appalling things, don't make the mistake of thinking I'm excusing them. Nor, in analysing morality in the way I have, am I seeking to invalidate it. All I'm arguing is that it's another human construct. As such, it's as much subject to all the same modulations as affect all other human affairs, along with all the accretions and diminutions you'd expect, and as likely as everything else to become muddled or obsolescent. In the last few centuries we've quite rightly come to think of slavery and racism as immoral, once we bothered to allow our empathy to break through to another circle of our fellow humans. However, for most of the period of recorded human history (what we call civilisation), slavery was simply an economic fact of life, while far more recently racism was an entirely respectable and latterly allegedly 'scientific' opinion held by decent and responsible people. But I'm not advocating some kind of temporal relativism here to justify the crimes of the past. Slavery and racism were and are evil. In previous times, as often happens, the evil wrought on other people was outweighed by the good accruing to the people in a position of power to do anything about it. The same truth

[12] Significantly, it's long been recognised that psychopaths lack any real sense of empathy, and invariably commence their careers in violence by being cruel to animals.

applies today, wherever you care to look across the human world, and in spades.

Of course, when many of the religiously minded talk about morality, they probably have something else in mind, and denying morality to other people is just one of the ways, by my definition, they set themselves off on the path to immorality. It's religions' tendency to assume that our capacity for bad behaviour is not balanced by an equally powerful and innate capacity for goodness, which they then insist can only be imposed from without, that I find so irritating and, for that matter, anti-human. As a species we're capable of hideous callousness and cruelty, on a tiny or enormous scale, but we're also capable of the opposite, and by and large we've policed ourselves for the last 200,000 years pretty efficiently, or we probably wouldn't be here and in such huge numbers.

Whether you want to put that down to living a moral life is up to you, but I really don't get it when one group of people starts hounding and persecuting any other group of people, particularly when they do so in the name of morality. I think you probably know what I'm talking about.

And that's something else I don't get about religion: why on earth (which is the only place we are or ever likely to be) do its subscribers constantly feel compelled to tell me and everyone else how to live my life?

I understand exactly why they do it though.

I've sought so far to outline what I believe is a correct analysis of the nature of human beings, and various consequences that have arisen from that nature. In doing so, I hope I've merely been restating the blindingly obvious, albeit with grand sweeping statements and massive generalisations.[13] Then again, I'm a caricaturist, although in defence of my profession I'd also insist that the point of caricature is to exaggerate things in order to make their true nature more obvious, a bit like a parable.

That said, by and large I subscribe to the opinion that other people can believe whatever rubbish they want to, so long as they leave me alone. But here, of course, is where religion in particular becomes a problem and not just an irritation. I know that there are secular Inquisitors out there

[13] For example, my ideas on empathy and projection will be familiar to anyone who has read the works of the German atheist philosopher and anthropologist Ludwig Andreas von Feuerbach. Unfortunately I haven't, although the fact that we come to the same conclusion is probably the result of the kind of unintentional plagiarism that beset George Harrison in his legal wrangles over the similarities between Harrison's 'My Sweet Lord' and The Chiffons hit 'He's So Fine'. More genuinely co-incidentally, Darwin and Alfred Russell Wallace came to the same conclusions about evolution at more or less the same time, although Darwin, as well all know, got to the printers first. Had it been the other way round, Richard Dawkins might now have been a Wallacian, although we can only speculate whether or not he would have endorsed Wallace's later obsession with spiritualism.

who will not rest until all error has been extirpated, and the last trace of, say, Rastafarianism has been wiped from the face of the planet. That, however, shouldn't really bother us. Religion is only truly a problem – in fact, only becomes of any wider importance – when it becomes a subset of politics.

So, moving on from the universal, let's narrow our focus down to the grubbily mundane, in order to make a case for claiming that more than being simply a subset, religion is, in fact, purely and solely political.

Look at it this way:

At some point in our human or prehuman history, as individuals we abrogated areas of responsibility to leaders, so that they'd do things for us, like protect us or make decisions on our behalf or take responsibility for a myriad other things we couldn't be bothered to do for ourselves. In return for these services, we allowed certain advantages to accrue to them, like first choice of mate, first snap at the tapir and so on. This, like empathy and consciousness, exists in many other social species, although in humans it's tended, like a lot of other qualities we share with other animals, to become overly embellished into an often bewildering complexity.

Whether you label them as alpha males or kings or CEOs or bishops doesn't really matter. The point remains that they exercise power over us, often with our complicity. Returning once more to the constant interplay and contradiction between our individual consciousness and our capacity for empathy, we've always found this an uneasy contract. Given our species' ability to think about such things, we recognise or extrapolate from the evidence how this arrangement is convenient but also unjust, unfair and inequitable. Much the same could be said about our contract, or covenant, with God, because in both cases, having given them an inch, they thereafter expect much more from us than was originally part of the bargain: things like obedience, respect and even love.

But again, like everything else, it's a system which has the engine of change and adaptation built into it. Neither a boss baboon, Louis XIV, Saddam Hussein nor Tony Blair will live forever, and their hold on power is constantly challenged in all sorts of different ways, some of which have become institutionalised over time, while others erupt spontaneously and violently. The hedgehog-owning Friedrich Engels and his friend Karl Marx famously postulated a template for this dynamic, in the celebrated line that all history hitherto is the history of class struggle. I'd elaborate that slightly, and say that all human history hitherto (and also henceforth) is actually the history of power struggle, an endless tussle for control in all its legion manifestations, either to retain power, usurp it or, just as importantly, to thwart it. This is a general definition of politics, which can also be described as the eternal struggle between freedom and order.

In this continual, never-ending dialectic (for want of a better word) each side grabs whatever weapons are to hand to advance its own cause, be it violence, negotiation, mockery and the rest of it. The dice are usually loaded on the side of the powerful against the powerless, but not always. One weapon the powerful frequently use is awe, and with it notions of majesty, pomp and deference. Something else used again and again has been the idea of divinity.

Throughout history the links of kingship to religion, and vice versa, have been so close that they become indivisible. This is without doubt quite intentional, and I can think of no system of monarchy that has not, at its heart, either claimed to be sanctioned by the divine or to be divine itself. By the same token (although I'm happy to be corrected) I can't think of any monarch, even of the most impeccably liberal Scandinavian kind, who admits to being an atheist or to be sanctioned in their status by science and reason alone. To give just one example, Revolutionary France attempted several experiments in state atheism, but Napoleon brought back God and had the Pope officiating as he crowned himself emperor.

We'll probably never find out which came first, the priest or the king. It's enough to guess that each used the other to augment their authority, combining the invisible mysteries of the supposedly spiritual with the harsh reality of temporal power in order to overawe and intimidate everyone else into obedience.

Moreover, if you look at the phenomenon of religion as augmenting temporal power, suddenly several of the things I said I didn't 'get' about it start making sense. Thus worshipping a deity stops being simply a rather simple-minded human response to natural phenomena you can't explain, and instead becomes a far more complicated, understandable, expedient and probably sensible display of subservience to the king, extended into the spiritual realm to compound yet further your feelings of subservience. And by extension the idea of blasphemy makes sense too.

I've always been puzzled by blasphemy, and why people get so worked up about it. If God exists as a being so powerful that he, she, it or they created everything in the first place, why should his, her, its or their followers be in the slightest bit worried about other people mocking or denigrating the focus of their beliefs? Surely God's big enough to look after him, her, it or themselves, without persons of faith humiliating themselves by burning books, closing down plays, trying to ban TV programmes or films or threatening to kill other people, and as often as not carrying out the threat for good measure. I know this is a flippant line of argument, but that doesn't invalidate it. However, if you see blasphemy less as a slight to God, and more as a kind of lese-majesty, or insult to the king, it all makes sense. Blasphemy is, I'd argue, just another of those political weapons used throughout human history to reinforce, retrench or claw back worldly or political power, and you can see this in operation wherever blasphemy becomes an issue.

For instance, in the loathsome fatwah announced against the novelist Salman Rushdie by Ayatollah Ruhollah Khomeini for his book *The Satanic Verses*, amidst the death sentence declared on Rushdie, the frenzied demonstrations throughout the Islamic world, the actual murders of Rushdie's publishers and translators committed in the name of Islam, everyone seemed to overlook a part of the novel which goes a long way to make sense of something which was so terrifying to the secular West because it seemed to make no sense at all. Halfway through the novel, Rushdie gives us a highly unflattering but also very funny portrait of an exiled Islamic cleric and the various humiliations and indignities he suffers, including the water temperature in his shower suddenly changing because one of his bodyguards flushes the toilet.[14] One of the things we should remember about Khomeini, but which we invariably forget as we mesmerise ourselves into an existentialist terror of Islam (exactly as we're meant to), is that when he originally returned to Iran after the overthrow of the shah's dictatorship he stated categorically that he had no intention whatsoever of playing a political role. As we know, he rapidly changed his mind, through a combination of vanity, arrogance and opportunism, and was soon exterminating his political enemies more effectively and with greater enthusiasm than the shah ever

---

[14] On the subject of personal hygiene, early on in his presidency Khomeini's political acolyte Mahmoud Ahmadinejad ordered the arrest of some young Tehranians who'd been texting each other that he was smelly because he never washed.

had. In this context, even if Khomeini failed to articulate it to himself, it seems to me that he was motivated as much by personal vanity, lese-majesty and political arrogance as by piety. Thus he was just the latest despot to recruit God to fight his personal as well as his political battles, just as despots have done for millennia, making the realities of worldly power not just awful but awesome too.

This is simply to state an historical truth, but also to point up a common political phenomenon: to identify a trans-cendent, extra-human dimension which determines human affairs to augment and strengthen your political stance, which then becomes inexorable and unavoidable and therefore unanswerable.

You can see this tactic used everywhere. In Marxism, Marx and Engels brilliantly synthesised a widespread political position – of general opposition to those in pos-session of power, interwoven with political reactions to the depredations and economic consequences of the Industrial Revolution – into what they described as a kind of 'science' which was therefore by definition 'true'. Evoking a deter-ministic version of History – in other words, an idea of History as an independent force more powerful than the individual people who lived it – they thus sought to strengthen their political agenda by saying that the out-come they sought – the triumph of the powerless over the powerful – was inevitable. There was also a secular kind of eschatology built into this model. Just like in the book of Revelation (a book added to the New Testament almost as an afterthought by its early editors), Marxism prophesied a future inevitability, and the Second Coming of Christ and the Triumph of the Proletariat both comfortingly predict the unavoidable final and utter defeat of your current enemies. This prospect of hope becoming certainty is what gave both Christianity and Marxist socialism their enormous potency, in all their various warring mutations and factions.[15]

You can find exactly the same tactic used in capitalism. Despite markets being made up exclusively of individual people interacting with each other, in order to achieve the political objective of retaining power and control, the 'Market' has been elevated into a transcendental force, quite beyond the control of humans who are therefore predestined to be tossed about according to its every latest caprice.[16]

[15] It's also worth noting the remarkable similarities between the First Council of Nicaea and the First International in the way they transformed tactics into strategies and policies into dogma. In the latter meeting we can see the Russian anarchist Mikhail Bakunin (Wagner's original model for the character of Siegfried) taking on the role of Presbyter Arius from the former, with both of them ending up expelled and anathematised. I could draw lots of different conclusions from that, although the one I prefer is the utterly human nature of both meetings, suggesting the equally human nature and source of their different agendas. Then again, you could compare both conclaves, with equal validity, with the vicious backbiting you'll find in your average amateur theatrical group and come to the same conclusions. It's also worth remembering that both socialism and Christianity constantly whittled away at themselves to produce the narrowest possible interpretation of orthodoxy, until what you ended up with bore little resemblance to what you had at the start. The Bolsheviks were just one of many specifically Marxist parties in pre-Revolutionary Russia, just like the Marxists were simply one strand of nineteenth-century anti-capitalism. The Bolsheviks just happened to be both more ruthless and more expediently willing to seize any available opportunity than any rival party, including the Social Revolutionaries who'd won the election in 1917 before Lenin staged his coup. Then came Stalin, who whittled even more away until Soviet socialism, in many people's eyes, came to look exactly like Gibbon's description of the state of Christianity after the Council of Nicaea: 'Thus they built a bridge to Heaven the width of a razor's blade, and all in the name of the God of Love.' As we know, Stalin then wielded the razor with a vengeance.
[16] Significantly, the chief apostles and devotees of the Market display

This compulsion to surrender ourselves to higher powers of our own creation, although both explicable and understandable, is still lamentable, and usually only serves to increase the ways in which we dehumanise ourselves and other people in order to control them and compel them to start making sense. Thus, while the religious may only see souls waiting to be squirted out of imminent carrion, scientists are just as prone only to see data, as are historians, statisticians, sociologists and many others too. Doctors of mind and body see pathologies or cases; capitalists see units of production or consumption; politicians see potential supporters or enemies; despots see enemies or scapegoats. And on it goes, despite the fact that all any of them ever really see are other people.

Well, that's politics, and so, to a large part, is religion. You can see it in the god-kings of the ancient world or Aztec Mexico or twentieth-century Japan. In Ancient Rome you could be deified by a vote in the Senate (and be de-deified too, once the political wind had changed direction). Even after the Emperor Constantine made Christianity the state religion of the Roman Empire, the emperors were still called 'divinity'. Charles I's blood, spilled on the scaffold in Whitehall, was held by many to be sacred, and a lot of the spectators dipped their hankies in it to grab some of the magic. Shortly before I wrote this book, Dr Rowan Williams stated categorically that Prince Charles' desire to be dubbed 'Defender of Faiths' during the ancient and ritualistic mummery of his prospective coronation was an absolute no-no: in other words, he's

absolutely no sense of shame whenever it's politically expedient to blaspheme against the hidden hand of their tacky god. When it comes to selling weapons to indolent Saudi princes or torture equipment to the vilest despots imaginable, manipulating the market is always justified as essential to maintain British jobs, despite the inconceivability of even the idea of bribing a coal mine.

Anglicanism's juju, and no one else's. But that brings me back to my earlier point about how religion only becomes of any importance when it takes on a political dimension.

Let's stick with Christianity. From its beginnings Christianity was a political religion, narrowly within the context of challenging the hierarchy of Jewish ecclesiastical politics, then more widely as an abstentionist ideology for the dispossessed, offering a programme of off-planet politics because it was in no position to do anything about the drains down here on earth. Nonetheless, for all sorts of reasons we've already seen, it proved highly alluring as it was slowly twisted out of recognition, in a series of political displacement activities (the invisible politics of rowing about doctrine is just as political as any other kind). However, it only became of any enduring importance once it became the state religion of the Roman Empire, which happened for reasons of political expediency. (For the record, it also exemplifies the universal way oppositionist movements have a tendency to become even more tyrannical than the tyrannies they displace, as we've already seen with Khomeini's reign of terror in post-Revolutionary Iran. This is because successful revolutionaries invariably add revenge to the rest of their political agenda.)

In this analysis, although it was the prospect of post-death political fulfilment which attracted the wretched into the parallel politics of Christianity, it was its doctrinal dimensions, and their entirely temporal application, which attracted Constantine. The notion of the Trinity, for instance, was a perfect template for the political circumstances the emperor found himself in at the time of the Edict of Milan which decriminalised Christianity throughout the Roman Empire. He was co-emperor, but aspired to be sole emperor. Either way, the riddle contained within the Trinity – to be single yet manifold, many yet one – provided a perfect metaphor whether Constantine was sharing the purple, or later when he succeeded in his political ambition in uniting what had previously been divided within his own person.

Similarly, the importance placed by Judaism on the physical city of Jerusalem had been transformed in Christianity into the *idea* of Jerusalem, and thereafter the hope of a new Jerusalem. You'll appreciate the importance such a revolutionary shift in sensibility could hold in a vast empire centred on another city, in this case Rome. Ideas are portable in your head: Rome, as an idea, had been exported throughout the known world; and yet the paganism that had previously been its state religion was largely predicated on physical locations rather than the idea of them. For whatever reason it was that these places were, and often remain, sacred, they are also static: the propitiations they demand are local and localised. However, the New Jerusalem is universal. Christians were specifically told, according to the chroniclers of their redeemer's words, that they could propitiate him wherever two or three of them were gathered in his name. Because Christianity, unlike many previous religions, is based on the *idea* of a location as opposed to the location itself, it had the potential to be universal, a potential it largely fulfilled. I believe it's no coincidence that in its Christianised form, the Roman Empire moved its capital to Byzantium, which became Constantinople, but which was also called the 'New Rome'. Thus you can see how aspects of Christianity fitted Constantine's political purposes like a glove.[17]

*

But Christianity was only able to fulfil its universalist potential

---

[17] This launched a classic dialectical dynamic, this time about the location of temporal authority. A generation after the capital of empire moved to Constantinople, Pope Leo the Great made a claim to be *primus inter pares* patriarch, having authority over the patriarchs of Antioch, Byzantium and so on, because of his physical location in Rome, the centre of a pagan empire which had prepared the ground for the eventual triumph of Christianity.

once it had political backing and started to cross-fertilise with its political sponsor, as the state reinforced the temporal authority of the religion and the religion increased the awe-inspiring spiritual dimensions of the state until the two became indivisible. For his part, it remains a matter of speculation whether or not Constantine was even baptised before he died. Meanwhile, the Christian Church flourished even as it tore itself apart in doctrinal disputes of the sublimest indifference in a classic act of displacement to abjure it from either political responsibility or blame, and reinforced its position by colonising the sacred sites and feast days and stealing the trappings and practices of the religions it also displaced.[18]

*

The divinity or otherwise of the being in whose name the Christian Church was founded is, as far as I can tell, largely irrelevant to its subsequent success. The same goes for Islam. Whatever the truth or otherwise of the origins of the Qur'an, it served as the perfect engine for expansionist Arab imperialism, both in uniting Arab tribes around a single, transportable idea, the potency of which was enhanced by the excruciatingly detailed instructions on personal behaviour that were central to it, and providing them with a bulwark against the encroachment of rival empires, from whose own religions it also freely borrowed.

Later, different mutations of Christianity served as engines of Spanish imperialism, then British and now American imperialism. Shintoism and a local variant of

[18] For the record, halos, eastward-facing altars and the date of Christmas Day were all stolen from Mithraism, as well as the doctrine of the Virgin Birth, while the idea of life after death was pinched from Zoroastrianism, and so on and on and on. To return for a moment to my much wider thesis, you can witness similar ecological behaviour between grey and red squirrels.

Buddhism served as engines for Japanese imperialism. In each case, an apparently spiritual dimension serves a purely political purpose. In some cases, like the Church of England, from the beginning there was no spiritual dimension whatsoever, it being wholly the creation of political expediency, and it flourished purely as an extension of state authority. Its present obsession with sex is a mark of its political weakness as it tears itself apart over the irrelevant in order to disguise its own utter irrelevancy. Likewise, as the result of generations of abject Arab political failure, Islam is probably as rancorous as it is because of its dwindling political importance.

Gandhi once said, 'those who think religion has nothing to do with politics understand neither religion nor politics'. Although he'd probably disagree passionately if non-violently with my take on that statement, I think Gandhi was right. Not only has religion got everything to do with politics, but it should be treated in exactly the same way.

*

As I've already suggested, throughout time people have buttressed their political ambitions, themselves a twisted plait of different motivations, with religion, whether those motivations are economic or tribal or ethnic or simply the timeless tyrannical urge to control other people the better to control and thus make sense of the world. Religion more or less suits all purposes, from justifying slavery to abolishing it, from building an empire to abandoning it, from subjugating other people to emancipating them, or from loving them to hating them.

Nor is all of this necessarily a bad thing. Again, in many ways, it's just another thing.

So, while I may not subscribe to their beliefs, I refuse to

take that as justification for condemning actions I otherwise
applaud merely because the people who carry them out
claim that they're motivated by religion. That includes
Buddhist monks fearlessly and selflessly opposing the
Burmese junta, the Methodist Donald Soper opposing
nuclear weapons, Martin Luther King[19] opposing racism,
Desmond Tutu fighting apartheid or millions of other
unknown, unnameable people whose acts of bravery or
charity arise, they believe, from their faith. Even though I
object strongly to the offensive and arrogant idea that good
deeds are impossible without religion, in the end, as far as
I'm concerned, the act outweighs the motivation.

However, when a harmful act is justified by the religious
sensibilities of the perpetrator, you have to take that as a
contributory factor, even if you accept the mitigating circumstances which often explain and invariably outweigh
any purely religious motivations.

For instance, I actively deplore the opinions of many
religiously minded citizens of the Mid-western states of
America on other people's sexuality or what women choose
to do with their bodies, even though I recognise that they're
as religious as they are, not because they're inherently
wicked or stupid, even though they may act accordingly as
a consequence, but because they live boring lives, far apart
from each other in a sparsely populated area where their
Church provides them with their one weekly chance to
socialise outside their family and seek out the fellowship
their humanity yearns.

To take another example, I utterly condemn the angry
young men who blow up themselves and others in the name

---

[19] Try as I might, I can't quite swallow Christopher Hitchens'
argument in *God Is Not Great* that King, because he was a good if
flawed man who did good and great things which Hitchens applauds,
wasn't actually a Christian at all, whatever he might have said or done
to the contrary.

of Islam, even though I suspect they do so not because of the existentialist nature of Islam itself or the fact that selective interpretations of its dicta either allow or demand their actions, but probably because the jihadist wing of Islamism provides the last credible political refuge for young men alienated by their circumstances, political forces beyond their control and the complacency and failure of their parents' generation. To that I'd add that, having the optimism and dreams that all young men everywhere have always had, they've been seduced by the romance of a futile gesture in the name of a great cause. A generation ago I suspect that they'd have been Marxists, a generation before that nationalists, and in either case, although less likely to kill themselves, they'd have been as likely to kill other people, as well as being willing and happy to die for their cause and still think that their actions were right and just.

But in all of those examples, my response is a purely political one, because the actions I'm applauding or deploring are themselves political and nothing else.

The problem – and I don't deny that there is a very real problem here – is that religion, in its political form, invariably insists that it is primarily religious and only political thereafter, and that the motivation will always outweigh the act, even though I believe, as I hope I've demonstrated, that exactly the opposite is actually the case.

*

What's really at issue here is the nature of the politics. In the distant past when religion first became an adjunct of political power, it was as part of an aspirationally totalitarian system, and its purpose was to complete the totality. The Ten Commandments may appear to be pretty straightforward in their brevity, but don't forget that they're

qualified by thousands of verses in Leviticus telling you
exactly how you should behave in every imaginable
circumstance.[20]

*

[20] As it happens, Chapter 11 of Leviticus allowed me to make my only
verifiable conversion. When I was about seventeen or eighteen, I went
round to my mate Neil's house in Ruislip to keep him company while
he babysat his eleven-year-old younger brother Martin. We were in
the sitting room drinking beer and probably smoking a joint or two
when Martin came down from his room, and for reasons I can't now
quite remember, I mischievously and rather unfairly asked him about
religion, and thereafter started reading him the chapter in Leviticus
about clean and unclean meats. To the uncomplicated adolescent, this
passage appears to be utterly arbitrary in its proscriptions, as well as
being almost anal in its nitpicking detail. (It was only later that parts
of it began to make sense: the proscription against eating pork is less
to do with the health implications and more concerned with
husbandry. A happy pig who will produce edible meat requires shade
and lots of mud to wallow in, for reasons of porcine dermatological
hygiene, and both requirements are in short supply in a desert. It's
sensible, therefore, to ban the beast altogether rather than waste your
time trying to rear it against the odds. Likewise, in the socio-economic
circumstances of India, a cow is far more valuable alive as it provides
a continued source of protein in the form of milk, rather than being
dead and making just a couple of meals, and so the animal's evolution
into sacredness was another effective way of saving you from making
a serious economic mistake. Every religiously based food taboo has, if
you look deeply enough, a sound and entirely mundane origin.)
Anyway, the other thing about Chapter 11 is that it's very funny, if
you approach it with the right degree of disrespect and read it out
loud in the right voice. Having done so, I thought no more of it until
several decades later at Neil's fortieth birthday party, when a slightly
portly, early middle-aged man came up to me and said he wanted to
shake me by the hand. It was Martin, who said that that one reading
from Scripture had revealed to him how ridiculous religion was, how
he'd been godless ever since, and now he wanted to thank me. That,
without question, is a result, even though Neil's and Martin's middle
brother, Duncan, remains a committed and sincere Evangelical
Christian to this day.

Anthropologists have argued that the point of having every aspect of life codified in such precise and exacting detail is, first, to overawe the recipients of the law with its scope and enormity, and second because this awe at the majesty of the law might, just possibly, make the people obey at least some of it. The prospect of eternal as well as temporal punishment is clearly another way of imposing order, to allow the smooth running of society. Again, this is an aspect of the endless conflict between order and freedom, between our individual consciousness and our empathy, and a society without any laws, be they written or understood, would be terrifying and unworkable, however initially attractive.

In many ways, the various codifications of law were simply the restatement, albeit massively over-embellished, of those innate modes of social behaviour with which we and other species effectively police ourselves anyway. After all, in reality the law of the jungle is as exact and exacting as the Code Napoleon. Nonetheless, there is something both chilling and faintly disgusting about those people who continue the process of abrogation of responsibility to higher authority and immerse themselves willingly and completely in the law. Although the law, like God or the market, is a human construct, it is not itself human but a machine. Complete obedience to it isn't human either, but in many ways a denial of our humanity, particularly when, having balanced out all the conflicting factors, we choose obedience and adherence to human laws over and above the harm they do to other people.

Although I've outlined at length how a vast array of different factors, within our natures and outside them, from our genes to our environment, predispose us to behave in certain ways, they emphatically do not predetermine us. We are, to be sure, creations of the circumstances and experiences of our past, and we're also genetic creatures, and biochemical and hormonal beings as well, but at the precise if forever transient point of the present – at this moment now – we exist in futurity as entirely free agents, albeit responsible for the choices and the judgements we make. Like the template of evolution, we bob and weave to meet each fresh expediency, and just because we're equipped in various ways to do that, it doesn't follow that the equipment dictates all our future actions.

Indeed, of all the irritating aspects of religion which human minds have fabricated, I find the doctrine of predestination the most odious and idiotic. As a narrative, I suppose it's quite amusing to believe that God created tiny creatures in the seas millions of years ago in order that, eventually, their bodies be transmuted into crude oil so that, thanks to Winston Churchill's decision to convert the way the British fleet was powered from coal to oil, a bunch of nomads who now live above where the tiny creatures once lived would become so enriched and corrupt it would lead one of their citizens to launch a campaign of terrorism to overthrow them which expanded into a never-ending war of attrition and rage to encompass everyone different from him, which in turn led directly or indirectly to the deaths, among others, of hundreds of thousands of Iraqis, *simply in order that I write this sentence.* Far less amusing is the idea that the appalling number of people who've died in recent years on pilgrimage to Mecca did so because either it was 'written' or because they were bad Muslims or just Muslims in the first place (as some people have insisted), when those deaths were the fault and responsibility of the complacent and criminally incompetent Saudi authorities.

Still, ducking responsibility by appealing to a higher authority or power is a depressingly frequent aspect of human affairs. During the Taliban's brief tenure of power in Afghanistan, the only member of its government to be interviewed on TV said that the most beautiful thing about

Islam was that the Qur'an told you what to think and how to act in every conceivable eventuality, which is one of the sincerest statements of complete abrogation of personal responsibility I've ever heard.[21] (Even though it may require extraordinary feats of exegesis to extrapolate from the verses of the Qur'an the quickest way to reload a Kalashnikov, this doesn't seem to have proved much of a problem.)

Nonetheless, I hope it was established long ago that obeying orders isn't a defence, and that applies wherever you might think the orders come from. Nor is this limited to blaming your god or your leaders. The common human proclivity for blaming other people has also had hideous consequences, as we've see all too often, particularly when we use this tactic to portray ourselves as victims. This is just another of the ways we claim that none of it's our fault. Remember that Nazism was rooted in the idea of victim-hood: the German people were victims of the 'stab in the back' by domestic traitors at the end of the First World War; they were victims of Bolshevism, Versailles, international bankers and the Jews; even their anthem, the Horst Wessel Song, idolised its author, a young, blond Nazi activist cruelly murdered by the wicked Communists. (Incidentally, the Nazis stole the tune from the Communists, who'd originally stolen it from the Salvation Army). This sense of victimhood was used to justify the most appalling period of sustained victimisation in history. But you then get a kind of domino theory of victimhood: the Jews were genuine victims of the Nazis, who weren't victims; however, the Israelis now victimise the Palestinians whose plight as victims themselves has inspired a pan-Islamic victimisation of Jews. This includes the president of Iran Mahmoud Ahmadinejad among many others denying that the Jews were ever victims at all, though the current levels of

[21] For the record, thanks to decades of warfare, the Taliban government was the most disabled in history. Make of that what you will.

paranoia in parts of the Islamic world suggest to me that Muslim Holocaust deniers do so because of what can only be called 'Holocaust envy'. In other words, they can't stand the fact that the Jews have got more victim points than they have. This is the only explanation I can think of to justify the Muslim Council of Britain's boycott of ceremonies to mark Holocaust Memorial Day for many years.

(Other Holocaust deniers, as well as being deeply sinister, are weirder, as the only people who believe what Goebbels would have called this 'Big Lie' are vicious anti-Semites who clearly wish it had happened anyway.)

What's truly unpalatable about this pervasive culture of victimhood is when the powerful use it to entrench their power. That includes men's groups beating drums and whingeing in response to feminism, or perennial grizzling about political correctness. And the Catholic Church is by no means alone among religions in the way it's traded for centuries on the sufferings of its martyrs, long after it started piling up the corpses of plenty of other martyrs from other faiths or from none. You can understand why they do this: it may be pitiful, but we're also predisposed to respond to the piteous. Even so, some years ago when the journalist Lynn Barber interviewed Richard Adams, the author of the rabbity epic *Watership Down*, I read her description of him breaking down in tears when he started talking about the Wounds of Christ with dismay and a certain amount of disgust. This was because personally I think that there are a whole bunch of better things for him to cry about. One of them might have been the fate of the Aztec prince who was burnt by the Inquisition after the Spanish conquest of Mexico and who shouted from the flames: 'I don't understand! Why do you have to kill me just because I don't think that God lives in a biscuit?'

*

The history of religion in its totalitarian form is strewn with atrocities, which are so well catalogued I don't need to repeat them here. In its attenuated form, as temporal power has slipped from its grasp, organised religion shows no sign of kicking the habit, and instead seeks other forms of political control. It was probably always its role, as an adjunct of state power, to terrorise the people into obedience and good behaviour across the board, using a variety of methods from promises of salvation or threats of damnation to institutionalised murder. But in fulfilling that role, as is often the case with any government that eventually works out the limits of its power, a great deal of this urge to power has been displaced into irrelevancy. Thus many religions' obsession with the minutiae of personal behaviour. Once upon a time, after the Restoration of Charles II, the Anglican Church, restored to its role as the theocratic wing of monarchy, would tie up Scottish Presbyterians to stakes below the high-tide mark, offering them the chance to accept the Thirty-nine Articles (that beautifully vague monument to political expediency) or drown. Nowadays, all that's left to them is the option of splitting asunder over gay priests. But even when the religious regain temporal power, they invariably stick to this obsession with the personal and ignore the wider issues, probably because they have no real idea how to cope with them. The president of Iran exerts far more energy in enforcing modes of personal behaviour, including sending snatch squads into Iraq to abduct gay teenagers in order to hang them, than he does in addressing his country's genuine concerns, having put it on record that 'economics is for donkeys'. This means he's denied himself any option except leaving his nation's thirty per cent inflation to God to sort out.

There's a nice story I heard about life under the Taliban in Afghanistan. After they'd seized power, a producer on

Kabul TV lost his job when the TV station was closed down. Solely because she was a woman, his wife was forced to give up her job too, and his daughter was forced to leave school for the same reason. So the three of them stayed indoors, biding their time until things got better, and in the meantime, for a quiet life, he acquiesced to each fresh mad edict from the Taliban. These included trying to grow a beard the length of two bunched fists and, presumably, not flying kites or playing chess. However, one day Osama bin Laden issued a new edict saying it was a Qur'anic obligation for all men to wear eyeliner, at which point the producer decided that enough was enough, slipped off in the night to join the forces of the Northern Alliance and thus played his part in liberating Kabul from the world's most perfect government. It must have been perfect, because it was ordained by God. This didn't stop its citizens from lynching every last foreign Islamist fighter they could lay their hands on.

You're probably familiar with this celebrated ditty by Humbert Wolfe:

> You cannot hope to bribe or twist
> Thank God! the British journalist.
> But seeing what the man will do
> Unbribed, there's no occasion to.

The same goes for humans in general, and it's worthwhile pausing for a moment in order to ask whether it's religion, or ideology in general, or just our natures that make us behave so abominably to other people. For example, had God chosen not to give his final prophecy to Mohammed, would a putative Ruhollah Khomeini, 1,500 years on, have spent a dull if fruitful life harvesting pomegranates, or would he have found something within the dogmas of Zoroastrianism to justify the persecution and murder of thousands of his fellow Persians?

This question is, of course, unanswerable. But returning to my metaphor of the concentric circles as a way of describing how we interact with each other, if we twist it a bit it can also accommodate something else about humans. In this version (which requires you to imagine the template as being extended into infinite layers of transparent concentric circles laid on top of each other, but overlapping, so what you see is a multitude of intersecting Venn diagrams) although you as an individual occupy the central circle in the first layer, in subsequent layers you occupy other circles, further and further away from the centre. This is how we exist collectively, in the perception of all the other individuals around us.

As our empathy extends from each of us in all directions, we know very well that some people will choose to direct it outwards, while others, choosing to see themselves as placed in one of the additional layers, and occupying one of the outer concentric circles, will always choose to direct their empathy inwards, towards the centre or the bull's eye of the circles, to the kings, the creeds, the grand narratives or the laws, rather than towards the periphery. In other words, they'll always choose to obey orders, whatever their source, and thus constrict their imaginations rather than think about the consequences of their obedience to other people and of their lack of imagination on their victims.

But enough, for the moment, of metaphors. Even when barbarities are justified post or ad hoc by religion, it's ridiculous to blame religion for all the world's evils. Indeed, one of the more ludicrous dimensions of the current slanging contest between religionists and secularists is this absurd pissing match over whether Hitler or Stalin or Mao Zedong's atheistically motivated forays into mass murder were worse than the Inquisition's religiously motivated ones. Unsurprisingly, this leaves aside any more nuanced analyses, like the fact that many of the Nazis identified themselves as pagans, and were inspired as much by a deranged kind of folklorism as they were by perverted science, or that Stalin was a failed seminarian who said he sought to engineer men's souls, which he tried to achieve with all the subtlety of a bodging plumber repeatedly whacking everything with a monkey wrench. It also ignores the fact that Mao was the first person to succeed in bringing monotheism to China, albeit involving worship of himself and his desperately banal pensées. Essentially, this argument is about as useful and meaningful as arguing how many angels can dance on a pin head, or how many geneticists can dance on a gene, or whether Christopher Hitchens is cuter than his religiously inclined brother Peter.[22]

But although this kind of haggling is both pointless and obscene, it highlights another all too human tendency, in

---

[22] Within the circles of the metropolitan chattering classes, this argument happens more often than you might imagine. A famous atheist feminist writer I know insists that Peter's cuter, because she says that if you were stuck on a desert island with him he'd catch you a fish and build you a shelter whereas, in the same circumstances, Christopher would eat you. Personally, I can never think of the Hitchens brothers without recalling the following story about Mike and Bernie Winters, a brothers double act who enjoyed considerable success and fame in the 1960s and 1970s. Early in their career they were booked to play the Glasgow Empire, traditionally and notoriously the graveyard of English comics working the variety circuit, because the Glaswegian audience resolutely refused to even smile at anything any English comedy act did. Anyway, it was time for the Winters to go to do their bit during the first house, and Mike came on stage, front of curtain, and started his shtick. He was met with total silence. Not even a glimmer of a titter. But, being a professional, he gamely carried on despite the waves of hostility emanating from the auditorium, until it came to the part of the act where Bernie stuck his head through the curtains, gurning wildly at the audience. This, too, was greeted with deafening silence, until a voice was heard from the third row of the stalls muttering, 'Oh fuck! There's two of them!'

this case our need for grand narratives, like religion, or ideology, or science, into which we can displace our responses to the unspeakable.

Many people are rightly appalled and angered by the incompetence, naivety, stupidity, arrogance, opportunism and cynicism, on both sides, which has led in recent years to the deaths of hundreds of thousands of Iraqi civilians. At the same time, in the Congo, four million people were killed in a vicious civil war, many of them in the most horrific ways imaginable, and yet practically nobody cares, and hardly anyone in the Western world noticed anyway. This isn't just because it didn't involve the United States or a British prime minister constantly flaunting his conscience on his dampish sleeve, but also because it wasn't part of any grand narrative we've chosen to recognise. Iraq fits neatly into the grand narrative of the 'War on Terror' or 'A Clash of Civilisations', whereas in the Congo rival warlords were slugging it out in local turf wars, often fought by child soldiers, over tribal differences, revenging ancient or modern wrongs or trying to take or keep control of the country's wealth of mineral resources. These include the minerals used to make mobile phones, so in part the slaughter of those millions of people was to make sure that you and I can watch a football match or a rap video on a tiny little telly in our latest generation Nokia.

In truth you could, if you chose, draw back, strip off the mask of religion and see all the murderous factors at play in the Congo – tribalism, revenge, natural resources – in the Iraqi conflict as well. Without necessarily the same richness of natural resources, the same thing could apply to the thirty-year mini civil war in Northern Ireland. The same goes for the former Yugoslavia. It applies again, with imported tribalism this time, and the natural resources close at hand, in the Israel-Palestine conflict, where a toxic broth of colonialism, displaced European politics, post-imperialism

(Christian, post-Christian, prehistoric and Muslim), geopolitics, superpower proxy wars, Third World fury and First World guilt has been poisoned even further by the religious dimension.[23] In both those last examples, it seems

[23] There are various things which should be noted about the Israel-Palestine conflict. First off, the current state of the division of the world into the supposedly warring factions we think divides it is, like everything else, pure chance. Up until the moment when President Truman decided to recognise the state of Israel after the end of the British Mandate in Palestine, against the advice of his Secretary of State and the State Department, there was the strong possibility that, without US support, Ben-Gurion and his government-in-expectation would have sought sponsorship from Stalin's Russia. There was certainly a synchronicity there: Israel was originally as much a socialist entity as a Zionist one, and had circumstances been slightly different, Israel might have become a Soviet satellite in the Middle East, with or without the US Jewish vote which clinched the matter in Truman's mind. Remember that large swathes of the American Establishment were profoundly anti-Semitic until comparatively recently, and they'd happily have fried the Jewish atomic spies Julius and Ethel Rosenberg just five years after the foundation of the state of Israel, as much for being Jews as being Commies. (If there are any jokes to be got out of the neo-cons, there's this one: what's the difference between a traditional Republican and a neoconservative Republican? The neocons let Jews into their golf clubs.) Anyway, try to imagine this alternative state of affairs, and try to conceive the consequent interplay between the commonality of interest between Arab anti-colonialism, Israeli socialism, shared internationalism and Soviet sponsorship of the progressive forces in the region, lined up against American and British sponsorship of the reactionary, feudal Saudis to protect their oil interests. As they say, there but for the grace of God. . . The second point that needs to be made is that the religion-isation of the conflict really does call for the shared, patriarchal God of Judaism and Islam to show His hand after all this time. They are His children, after all, so it's about time He came down in glory and said that their behaviour had spoilt it for everyone, so He was going to impose a no-state solution, withdrawing His promise to everyone involved and instead allow this miserable strip of scrubland to be grazed by scimitar-horned oryx as part of His divine contribution to wildlife conservation. The third and final point to make is that because

to be the religious aspect that titillates us the most. Perhaps this is because religion is so mysterious, so irrational, so confused in its simultaneous declaration of universal love and reinforcement of tribal hatred and therefore so tantalisingly pervy. Maybe it's because it clicks with some ancient race memory in our id of the sexual thrill of big, brutal men beating the shit out of each other for no other reason than that they can. Either way, religion always seems to be the money shot in the Warnography that the twenty-four-hour news media ceaselessly serves up to us. These are conflicts based in tribalism, economics and geography, to which the combatants have added the apparently entirely irrational dimension of religious extremism to give them the edge in grabbing our attention. Unquestionably, we're appalled and fascinated (probably because we're appalled) by the irrationality of extreme human behaviour, all of which reminds me of the right-wing American journalist P. J. O'Rourke's best joke: say what you like about the Nazis, but no one ever had a sexual fantasy about being tied to a bed and whipped by someone dressed up as a social democrat.

*

If, as I hope I've demonstrated, religion has part of its origins and subsequently operates in a political context, the same has to be said for anti-religion too. The kind of atheism now widespread or even prevalent in many parts of the Western world owes far less to our awakening to the truths revealed by reason and science than to a much older tradition of anti-clericalism. Just as Marx and Engels formulated a 'scientific'

of the profligate burning of the oil owned by the Saudis down the road, the whole place is going to be under fifty feet of seawater in a hundred years' time anyway, so in the long term it all becomes rather academic.

analysis which they could then use as a weapon to achieve their political ends, so the Enlightenment provided the spur to accelerate and also to justify a pre-existing political struggle.

Anti-clericalism is just another aspect of that eternal and confused political human battle between the powerful and the powerless, the leaders and the led. Given the totalitarian context of much of the history of humanity we know about, it follows that frequently if not usually anti-clericalism was not only not an attack on religion as such, but within its political and historical context took the form of attempts to save religion from the elite who were perverting it. John Ball, one of the leaders of the Peasants' Revolt in England in 1381 and author of the revolt's still inspirational rallying cry, 'When Adam delved and Eve span, who was then the Gentleman?' was himself a priest. And yet the rebels had no compunction in beheading the then Archbishop of Canterbury because of his political crimes in advocating the poll tax which had sparked the revolt in the first place. Similarly, the Protestant Reformation was about smashing the power of the priests whose worldiness had deformed Christianity and then 're-forming' it from the first principles as laid out in the Gospels, although it ended up undermining the power of religion itself.[24]

---

[24] A salutary variant on this can be seen in the career of the Jacobin tyrant Maximilien Robespierre, who started off as a pious and sensitive child and grew up to be a champion of liberty who abhorred the death penalty. Described by Carlyle as 'seagreen incorruptible', he became so jealous of his own rectitude and virtue that he happily sent his best friends to the guillotine, rather than be thought of as anything except rigorously impartial in the exercise of revolutionary justice. However, despite his attitude to the Church and the libels of his enemies on the right, he was anything but an atheist. He dumped the young republic's new atheism and organised in its place the rather ridiculous Feast of the Supreme Being, and was particularly incensed by those extreme republicans who took to daubing the wonderful slogan 'DOWN WITH ETERNAL SLEEP!' on the walls of cemeteries. Among the last words

The initial success of Luther's Reformation was entirely dependent on political good luck and, as is invariably the case, good timing. Receiving the support of the German princes as a weapon with which to fight their ongoing political battles with the Holy Roman Emperor (in exactly the same way as Henry VIII created the Anglican Church in his battle with the Pope), Luther prospered where previous heretics, like John Hus, had failed for want of powerful political patronage and the invention of the printing press. But having succeeded in fracturing the monopoly of orthodox religion, the cracks continued to spread outwards exponentially. As a hundred flowers of reformation bloomed, they often also sought to choke each other to death as they rowed about authority. So thereafter you got Calvin, who advocated theocratic authority, and the Swiss theologian Thomas Erastus, who advocated the supremacy of the secular state; and the mushrooming number of Protestant sects were endlessly defying the most recent priesthood to emerge. The English Civil Wars started out as a battle between two different interpretations of Anglican Protestantism, albeit inextricably intermeshed with more general political struggles between rival claims to supreme temporal authority, but they ended up with a myriad Nonconformist dissenting sects, from the Ranters to the Muggletonians, fighting the Calvinist Presbyterians, and Oliver Cromwell bellowing the memorable line at the Battle of Dunbar, 'I beseech you, in the bowels of Christ, think it possible you may be mistaken!'

But there was another, theological dynamic that ran parallel to the more clearly political one. The best way to explain this is to repeat an example of that rare and

he addressed to the Convention before being arrested and guillotined in his turn were these: 'We will efface from our tombs your sacrilegious epitaph, and replace it with the consolatory truth, DEATH IS THE BEGINNING OF IMMORTALITY.'

beautiful thing, the Jewish-Irish joke. This is the one about the Jew walking down the Falls Road during the Troubles, who keeps on getting stopped at their rival roadblocks by the UDA or the UDF or the Provos. Each time he's stopped, he's asked if he's a Catholic or a Protestant, and each time he answers that he's a Jew. And, of course, his interrogators always reply, 'Yes, but are you a Catholic Jew or a Protestant Jew?' The same question can be asked of atheists, because there is a world of difference between a Catholic atheist and a Protestant one.

Catholic atheists, as we know from the wealth of literature written by them, are very strange, rather obsessional people who, in rejecting God, have rejected *everything* at once, dumping God along with all the other trappings of the universal and universalist Church. Left in a state of shock, they're doomed to go on and on about it for the rest of their lives, a bit like Graham Greene. A Protestant atheist, on the other hand, having already made the first move of discarding the dogma of the authority of the Pope, is free to continue discarding dogma, be it transubstantiation, belief in the intercession of saints or the truth of the Trinity, until he or she ends up blithely rejecting the dogma of belief in God, and with no apparent ill effect. It's a bit like the difference between leaping from the deck of the *Titanic* and landing with a crippling bellyflop in the icy waters eighty feet below, or waiting til the deck reaches sea level and stepping effortlessly into the waiting lifeboat. After all, whoever heard of a lapsed Anglican?

But there was a third dynamic at play as well. The fracturing of what had been called Christendom led directly to over 200 years of almost permanent European warfare. There were the Wars of Religion in France, England's endless wars against Spain after the Pope had excommunicated and anathematised Elizabeth I and said her assassination was now a godly duty, the Thirty Years War and the English Civil Wars, among many others. But see how two of those wars ended.

Some historians have claimed that in terms of civilian deaths the Thirty Years War was proportionately the most brutal and deadly European conflict until the Second World War, with up to thirty per cent of the German population dying either as a direct consequence of military action or through the famine and disease that came in its wake. The war had been started by the Holy Roman Emperor's conviction that the souls of his Protestant subjects were of more importance than their bodies. When it was finally concluded at the Peace of Westphalia in 1648, possibly millions of corpses later, the protagonists merely reaffirmed the principles of the Peace of Augsburg of 1555, the status quo before the war which had stated that each state's religion would be determined by its prince. But, more significantly, they didn't bother to invite the Pope, in whose name the emperor had been acting with such dire consequences.

Forty years later in England, and forty years after the end of the civil wars which had resulted in the deaths of a tenth of the population of the British Isles, the issues which had led to those wars had still not been resolved. At the time of the Catholic James II's flight[25] in 1688, the three major factions – the High Church Anglican Tories who believed in the Divine Right of Kings, the Low-Church Anglican Whigs who wanted to hobble the power of the king and exercise it themselves, and the Nonconformist Commonwealth men of the Good Old Cause who'd got rid of the king altogether – had reached stalemate. More importantly, each recognised that none of them could win. After the arrival in England of James' nephew and son-in-law William of Orange, these parties met in secret conclave

[25] One reason why James fled, vacating the throne in the face of almost universal opposition to his regime, was that he had a nosebleed that lasted for three days.

and came to an agreement, the full details of which we still don't know, but which resulted in the Act of Settlement, the Act of Toleration, the Bill of Rights, and thereafter the suspension of press censorship, the development of the party political system and parliamentary democracy, freedom of conscience, freedom of expression, freedom of the press and, ultimately, the kind of liberal democracy which we continue, I hope, to enjoy.

What they did, in essence, was to act contingently, and to adapt to meet the circumstances they found themselves in. You could argue that they abandoned their principles, and nor were they motivated by any ideas of the kind of universal brotherly love advocated by the original founder of their different interpretations of Christianity. But you don't need to negotiate peace treaties with the people you love, except when love turns on a pinhead into hatred and you start tearing chunks out of each other through the courts over custody of the cat. In fact, they never stopped hating each other, but crucially they agreed to divert those hatreds away from the wars none of them could win into other channels, like adversarial parliamentary politics, blistering rows, bile, satire and much else besides. In short, in one of the more beautiful moments in human history, they didn't agree to agree, but agreed to stop killing each other because they knew they'd never agree.

In a revelatory moment, all these warring forces finally worked out that the total victory they yearned for, which would allow them to implement the totalitarianism each thought God had differently decreed, would elude them forever. So instead they acquiesced to be held in a kind of perpetual gravitational orbit around each other, rather in the way that Isaac Newton had recently described vast bodies in the heavens, held in their place by circumstances yet greater than their own. For his part, Newton was a

Unitarian and harboured all sorts of weird opinions and
beliefs about all sorts of things, but his observations, maybe
despite himself, offered a description of the heavens which
ultimately lacks a god.

The point about both the Peace of Westphalia and the Act
of Settlement was that both were part of a fourth, parallel
dynamic which established that religion was a secondary
consideration. When the level of human carnage finally
became intolerable, then tolerating the people you hate –
not agreeing with them, or appeasing or loving or even
liking them – was by and large preferable.

*

In the sweep of European history these four different but
linked dynamics all played a part in diminishing religion,
by fracturing its temporal authority, questioning its
spiritual authority, neutralising it as a cause of conflict and
consequently downgrading its importance until the fourth
dynamic works itself out and religion becomes, for many
people, of no importance at all. If you're interested in cause
and effect, you can thus see a clear line of descent from the
Reformation to the Enlightenment.[26]

[26] Working backwards, you could also argue that the Black Death
paved the way for the Reformation. Having killed off half the
population of Europe in the 1340s, the plague made the totalitarian
structures of feudalism inoperable, leading to what Engels described
as 'the Golden Age of the Working Man'. It also led many to question
the efficacy of the Church, and the many millenarian cults that
emerged in the plague's wake were all fundamentally anticlerical.
This informed the climate which made Luther's Reformation both
possible and successful. It was the Reformation which also allowed
for the development of capitalism, which led to Communism as well
as European mercantile imperialism. When the Catholic Church was
agitating for Christianity to be enshrined in the proposed European
Constitution a year or so ago, to recognise its role in shaping

It is the idea of tolerating it, rather than opposing it, which is ultimately fatal to the kind of totalitarian, political religion I've been describing. When mere men decided, for political expediency, to abandon the principle of the imposition of religious orthodoxy in the furtherance of political control (which was the standard political template in most of Europe at the time) it made that kind of religion unviable. I presume, because that's what I've been repeatedly told, that one of the main points of religion is that it provides you with a path to salvation or, more correctly, *the* path to salvation. Christianity in particular has been riven since its beginnings by mutually hostile, alternative interpretations of what that true path is. By definition they are incompatible. But if you have the truth revealed to you by God no less, you can't have a doctrinal smorgasbord, a marketplace of vying orthodoxies to pick and choose from. If you believe such things, the point of them is that they should be absolutely true. Moreover, as these things are the most important things ever, both personally and universally, they should therefore be worth fighting and dying for. Which explains the history of Christianity for at least one and a half millennia; it also explains the unfolding history of parts of Islam. And yet in 1688 a bunch of Englishmen decided among themselves that religion was no longer worth fighting and dying for.

It became secondary to public order. It became, very obviously, subservient to politics, and having lost its temporal power, it began to spiral away into irrelevance. As I said earlier, once it was no longer in a position to torture dissidents to death, the Church of England became a bit of a joke, its clergy famously the repository for the idiot sons of

'European civilisation', I felt that they should have enshrined the role of the bubonic plague bacillus instead. In fact they should go further, and erect a vast and monstrous statue of it in the middle of Brussels, if needs be knocking down a cathedral or two to make way for it.

the gentry, and fit only to people Trollope novels or *The Vicar of Dibley*, browbeat the poor, organise fetes and produce an unbroken succession of apostles of asininity. Christopher Isherwood, speaking of Archbishop Fisher's stance during the Abdication Crisis, said it for all of them: 'O Cantuar! How full of Cant you are!' And although at the time it was directed specifically against the Methodists, that latest fractured Christian groupuscule to assail the latest religious orthodoxy, when they cast the legend 'GOD BLESS THE CHURCH OF ENGLAND AND DOWN WITH ENTHUSIASM!' on a church bell in the middle of the eighteenth century, its message was timeless.

What this means in practice, in most of Britain, is that we have a Protestant state religion which, thanks to Henry VIII, proved at the moment of its creation that religion was subservient to politics. This was achieved without anyone suffering any noticeable divine retribution (unless his corpse exploding in its coffin has, in the long term, denied Henry the certain hope of the resurrection of the body). Protestantism contained the seeds of its own destruction, and in its Anglican incarnation was helped on its way by the Glorious Revolution which, in establishing the principle of tolerance, pushed religion even further down the scale of importance. The Enlightenment and Darwin helped do the rest, by demonstrating that the priesthood was staffed by liars as well as fools.

So while many of us still pay lip service to the trappings of religion, and manage to live reasonably happily with church weddings, horoscopes and yoga without any of them intruding too greatly on how we choose to live our lives, today most of us now know nothing of religion, don't understand it, don't really care for it and, most of all, are acutely embarrassed when confronted with it. Which is why our deeply pious former prime minister Tony Blair always

chose not to talk about his faith, including refusing to
answer Jeremy Paxman when he repeatedly asked whether
or not Blair had prayed in the Oval Office with George W.
Bush. It was because it would have made him a laughing
stock. Worse still, it would have been the squirming
laughter of deep embarrassment.

And this is the reason we tend to respond in such mixed
ways when the few religionists in our midst start
getting assertive. After a centuries-long process of de-
Christianisation, most of it arbitrary and by and large
accidental, we simply don't understand this thing well
enough to know exactly what to do when it or other
religions start getting chippy.

For instance, 400 years ago the news of the imminent
death of a Pope would have been greeted in England by
bonfires the length and breadth of the kingdom in cele-
bration of the joyous news that the Antichrist would soon be
burning in hell. And yet in 2005 the imminent death of John
Paul II was greeted by the British media with blanket
coverage, dripping with mawkish deference. This wasn't
because most of us care but because, I suspect, the people
who decide news agendas, not really understanding what
the Pope was, thought it safer to accord him a lot of airtime,
just in case someone somewhere objected if they didn't.
(And, of course, it filled potential dead air in the ravenous
schedule of twenty-four hour news.) In a way this was a
rather laudable motive. The news people were trying to be
nice, trying to be polite and inoffensive; and anyway, in
their eyes the Pope was just a nice old chap in a funny dress
of whom we knew little and cared less. In his irrelevance he
could, therefore, be imbued with those qualities we
invariably invest in the powerless and irrelevant; he could
be sentimentalised and infantilised into harmlessness in the
same way we treat the Royal Family, celebrity soap stars,
our children and our pets. So, for fear of giving the

possibility of offence, it was safer all round to ooh and aah and brush away tears of the purest humbug, and certainly make no mention of the millions of people who'd suffered in various ways, from AIDS or persecution or repression, thanks to the dictates of this rather wicked old man.

Our bewilderment goes across the board. In other times, in other circumstances, the suicide bombings on the London Underground on 7 July 2005 might have led to vicious pogroms against Britain's Muslim population. Thankfully they didn't, but it's worth asking why. Part of it was down to Londoners' rather grumpy native fatalism. Most of us knew that this was coming, being better able to recognise cause and effect than our then prime minister, whose religion teaches him that faith can move mountains, albeit with the assistance of thousands of tons of American high explosive. My then sixteen-year-old son was in Central London that morning, on his way to a work-experience placement in Hammersmith. When, to my immense relief, he finally got home, his first comment to me was, 'Was that it?' He, like the rest of us, had been primed by government and the media to expect something far more cataclysmic, and from the window of the room where I'm writing this I can see Lewisham's Citibank building, left empty by its owners as a potential bolt hole if Central London becomes permanently irradiated. That said, the response of Londoners to those murderous, misguided young maniacs was surprisingly muted, and even rather jokey. On 8 July a sentimental American opened a website called 'I am a Londoner and Today I hurt' which was soon inundated by messages like 'I'm a real Londoner and today I got the day off work.' I don't believe that this kind of thing was motivated by any sense of forgiveness, and certainly not by any kind of tacit approval. It was more like incomprehension tempered by resignation. Other nations, at other times, might have met an appalling provocation wrought in the name of a great world religion altogether more robustly, pilloried a few unrepentant imams before sewing them into pig skins at Tyburn and then carpet-bombed Mecca.[27] We didn't even begin to think of doing anything along those lines, and I'm rather proud of that. Nor did we open another front in the War on Terror. In fact, apart from the government attempting to introduce some even more draconian legislation than we already had, as a city and as a country we did nothing. Unlike the godly Americans, who responded to 9/11 by launching a global and never-ending war, the godless British actually followed the teachings of the founder of a religion they've largely abandoned, and more or less turned the other cheek.

*

Of course some people deplore this kind of feebleness in the face of what they called 'Islamofascism'.

Of itself, Islamofascism is an excellent and effective insult, although it's directed less at the jihadis and more at their Western fellow-travellers. In fact, as a political construct Islamism and its jihadi wing are pre-fascist by a long way, and are fighting to re-establish the Abbasid caliphate destroyed by Genghis Khan's grandson Haluga.

To digress for a moment, when the Mongol armies besieged Baghdad in 1258 they offered the caliph al-Musta'sim their standard terms: accept Mongol suzerainty

[27] It was not always thus. Before revenging itself at the Battle of Omdurman for General Gordon's death in the Sudan thirteen years earlier, the British Empire sent a flotilla of gunboats up the Nile as far as Khartoum, which then repeatedly shelled the tomb of the so-called Mad Mahdi Mohammed Ahmad until it was dust. And just to help its sales among the book-burning market, it shouldn't be forgotten that in *The Shape of Things to Come* H. G. Wells describes, with obvious approval, how the Air Dictatorship, his imagined oligarchy of technocrats of the future, bombs Rome and Mecca with nerve gas.

and swear fealty to the Great Khan or have your city destroyed and all its inhabitants slaughtered. The caliph responded rather rashly, it's said, by declaring that he couldn't possibly accept these terms as his god was better than the Mongols' gods. In spite of its subsequent reputation for unrestrained barbarism, the Mongol Empire exercised complete religious tolerance among its subject peoples, and Christians, Muslims, Buddhists, Confucians and Jews all attained high office under Genghis Khan and his successors. Haluga, however, is reported to have been so incensed by this declaration of intolerance that he personally kicked the caliph to death, sacked Baghdad, killed 90,000 of its inhabitants, burned its famous library and thus not only destroyed the great Islamic Empire, but also, centuries later, at least partially inspired Osama Bin Laden and his supporters to launch their careers of sanguinary nostalgia. For the record, Haluga was the last of the Mongol khans to have had human sacrifices at his funeral.

Al Qaeda's wider campaign against the West in general and the United States and its allies and satellites in particular – described by Tony Blair as 'existentialist' just to make it even more terrifyingly incomprehensible – is not so much a clash of civilisations as a bitch slap between a dead empire and a decadent one. More specifically, their campaign is against the corruption of the ruling House of Saud in Arabia, a battle fought within the parameters of Wahhabism, the harsh and unforgiving branch of Sunni Islam which its founder, Mohammed ibn Abd-al-Wahhab, guaranteed would prosper after its inception in the eighteenth century by actively seeking and receiving the sponsorship of the House of Saud. The spread of Wahhabism in the twentieth century is almost entirely thanks to the discovery of oil beneath the Arabian peninsula in 1932 and its subsequent ownership by the Saud family, which has bankrolled religious schools, outreach organisations, the suppression of Sufi shrines and a great deal else besides in order to promote their court religion.

Once again we see religion as the lackey of temporal power, which in its turn is being assailed from within by people seeking to save the religion from the corruption of its temporal and political protectors. Al Qaeda's wider campaign is almost certainly a consequence of the marked failure of their initial one to displace the Saud family, so they've engaged in a standard displacement activity instead, and are now attempting to rebuild a political edifice dead 800 years by small if deadly acts of wanton criminality against total strangers, and by attacking every other alternative branch of Islam within range. They justify their actions by referring to yet another grand historical narrative, just like the Serbs did when they unleashed their genocidal campaign against Muslim ethnic Albanians in Kosovo in 1999, to avenge the death of the Serbian King Lazar fighting against the Ottoman Turks at the Battle of Kosovo on St Vitus' Day in 1389.

*

Despite the fact that Al Qaeda and its allies and supporters happily concede that they are nothing but totalitarian theocratic imperialists, they have many apologists in the West. I suspect that this is because a lot of people on what is loosely called 'the left' are prepared to salute anyone who scores a palpable hit against their traditional enemy, the old enemy of Marx and Engels, now embodied by American capitalism. A few decades ago many young people, rightly horrified by the actions of capitalist imperialism in South-East Asia, both applauded and identified with the Stalinists running North Vietnam, the last group of underdogs effectively to humble the Americans. Some of those young people, older now, currently hold high office in the British government.

Christopher Hitchens, another of them and responsible for popularising the term 'Islamofascist', wrote an article in the *Observer* a while ago seeking to demonstrate the absolute difference between the actions of the Viet Cong and the activities of the Islamist insurgents in occupied Iraq. Hitchens' great hero, the Pomeranian-loving Leon Trotsky, made the point rather well: 'History has different yardsticks for the cruelty of the Northerners and the cruelty of the Southerners in the [American] Civil War. A slave-owner who through cunning and violence shackles a slave in chains, and a slave who through cunning and violence breaks the chains – let not the contemptible eunuchs tell us that they are equals before a court of morality!' That said, the point may have been lost on any South Vietnamese businessman grown rich on contracts with the US Army as he was led off into the countryside for 're-education' after the fall of Saigon, and it's probably equally lost on people in Baghdad either blown to bits by Islamist suicide bombers or blown to bits by the Pentagon's tactic of 'shock and awe'.

Drawing such a parallel is, of course, my error. I'm engaging in 'cultural relativism', one of the cardinal sins according to that Gadarenic crew of former British lefties who see support for or opposition to the Iraq War as the final point of no return. Personally, I'm surprised a lot of them never noticed, when they still identified themselves as either 'liberals' or were paid-up members of groupings far further to the left, that they were constantly surrounded by putative dictators or commissars, obsessives, opportunists, maniacs, lackeys, idiots, wimps and sell-out merchants capable of any betrayal so long as it suited their purposes, but there you go. All that really needs to be said about Iraq in this regard is that it was probably the right war fought by the wrong people at the wrong time.

Still, at the 2002 Labour Party Conference I went to a
rally where Hitchens was speaking, and listened to his
articulate and passionate plea that we show solidarity with
our socialist comrades in Iraq by supporting any action to
free them from Saddam's tyranny. It was a compelling
performance, and when I found myself standing next to
Hitchens in the Gents afterwards, I told him it was a highly
seductive notion, this idea of using the US imperium
under   Bush, Rumsfeld and Cheney as the patsy to
establish International Socialism around the world. I then
asked him how he proposed to find his moral high ground
when he kept on digging. Alas, before he could answer
(we'd now left the lavatories) the then Foreign Office
minister and former Bennite Chris Mullin came up to us
and said 'Hiya Hitch! Fancy a drink?' and they were gone
before I got my answer. To his credit, on his way out
Hitchens did turn back to me and give me a high five,
saying 'Stay cool!' as he did so.

But we mustn't get too bogged down in Iraq, even though
everyone else is, militarily, intellectually and emotionally.
Suffice it to say that the disaster in Iraq has merely upped
the ante for both sides, as all sides have behaved as
barbarously, callously and stupidly as it's possible to
imagine, right there in the cradle of civilisation.

But it's also shown just how adaptable human beings
can be, twisting and turning to meet each new circumstance, and choosing and discarding both allies and
ideologies as required. Thus Sunni Ba'athists, who'd
previously happily executed Islamists threatening their
power base, are now sponsoring the apparently limitlessly
expendable junior ranks of Al Qaeda or its local franchises
in an attempt to win it back, and Christopher Hitchens, the
deadliest exposer of the geopolitical crimes of American
imperialism under the stewardship of Henry Kissinger, is
now allied with its latest, crassest avatars in the shape of

an American Administration which shows every sign of being run as a racket by the Corleone family, but where they made Fredo the godfather instead of Michael.

By the same token lovers of liberty like the bear-owning Lord Byron or William Hazlitt championed Napoleon Bonaparte, a warmongering tyrant who created police states across Europe; the Fabians championed Stalin's Russia (while their contemporaries across the political divide in the British Establishment cheered on Hitler and Mussolini); future Cabinet ministers had little holidays in their hearts when Leninist totalitarians conquered South Vietnam; contemporary leftists condone the actions of Islamist imperialists because they hate American imperialism more. In each case an individual judgement is made, that an expedient alliance against a common foe outweighs the unpalatability of your current ally (and when I went on the Anti-war March in London on 15 February 2003, the thing that struck me most of all was the diversity of the marchers, and I wondered, if things worked out in their favour, who among the Stalinists, Trots and Islamists would kill the others first). This also explains Israel's continued and successful survival surrounded by its deadliest enemies: the Arabs hate each other more than they hate the Israelis, while the Israelis, who have an infinite capacity for hating each other – to the point where the only Israeli prime minister to be assassinated was killed by another Israeli – still manage to hate the Arabs more than they hate one another. And don't forget that within a month of the fall of Christian Constantinople to the Ottoman Turks in 1453, a rival Turkish sultan in Anatolia formed an alliance with the Venetian Republic against his Ottoman co-religionists.

But these are and were entirely political struggles, and you fight them with whatever weapons you have to hand.

Hurling the insult 'Islamofascist'[28] is one of them. Accusing those who question the cack-handed imperialism of the Americans of 'moral relativism' is another, despite the fact that labelling alleged appeasers of Islamofascism like that actually allies the accusers with the Islamofascists themselves, for whom the idea that their culture is equal to other people's is as alien to them as it was to the caliph kicked to death by Haluga.

Moreover, it's especially true that, when you're defending liberal democracy from its avowed enemies, you take particular care in watching out for what kind of politics the vigour of your defence leaves you with.

So it's all very well laying into Aunt Sallies like political correctness or multiculturalism, but what do you want in their place? Leave aside for the moment the fact that the tyrannous yoke of so-called political correctness, apart from apparently having the inbuilt propensity of a March hare for going mad, essentially just deprives people of their precious freedom to call black Britons niggers, British

[28] As I've already said, the point of the insult is to shame anyone on the left who's minded to offer comfort or support to Islamists by invoking the old enemy of fascism. The Islamists, one presumes, don't care one way or another. I experienced something simliar when I had a cartoon published in the *Guardian* in the summer of 2006, about the disastrous Israeli incursion into Lebanon intended but failing to destroy Hizbullah, 'The Party of God'. The cartoon was, I admit, graphically violent, reflecting the violent events it commented on in its criticism of the Israeli action, but I got as good as I gave when I started to recieve thousands of emails in a campaign initially orchestrated by the *Daily Mail* columnist Melanie Phillips through her website. 'Fuck off you antisemitic cunt' more or less summarises the content of most of them, doing the usual trick of equating criticism of the State of Israel with a general hatred of all Jews. I reject this accusation absolutely, though I recognise its effectiveness as both an insult and a tactic. And it worked. I was deeply shaken at being accused of something I'm not, which was the point of the insult. After all, if you'd said the same thing to Julius Streicher he might have cavilled at the cunt bit, but wore his anti-Semitism with pride.

Asians pakis or British Jews kikes, in public at least. You
should also forget that another way of looking at multiculturalism is as a classic liberal con job: the instinctively
racist British Establishment (not least in the subsequently
ironic form of Enoch Powell when he was Health minister)
originally encouraged 'new' Commonwealth immigration
to fill low-paid jobs in public transport and the Health
Service, but did nothing to either welcome the new arrivals
or to make their lives easier. That was left to well-meaning
liberals and other progressives who started promoting the
idea of the worth of the immigrants' cultural identity to
compensate for the fact that almost all they'd got in return
for their cheap labour was racism, poverty and deprivation.
This inevitably involved a deal of overcompensation, which
has now ossified into a deadening kind of bureaucracy (like
the utterly commendable motivations behind Health and
Safety legislation). However, the underlying message
remains 'You are going to do all the shit jobs that we can't
be bothered to do anymore, and in return we'll let you wear
your funny clothes and worship your silly little gods just so
long as you keep relatively quiet about it.'[29]

If there is a problem, it's that the second and third
generations aren't keeping quiet anymore. Young British
Asians are looking with disgust at a host society which
denies them opportunity and which treated their parents or
grandparents with barely disguised contempt and inhospi-
tality. They probably look at their parents with contempt
too, for doing nothing about it and instead keeping
themselves to themselves. What some members of this latest

[29] In the current climate of loud and public agonising over multi-
culturism, more and more people are advocating pro-active
programmes of reinforcing 'British Identity', with a lot of talk about
pledges of allegiance and so on. This unfortunately ignores the fact that
you've proved your 'Britishness' when you're unable to stop yourself
pissing yourself laughing at displays of fatuous earnestness like that.

generation have now done is to seek a route out of their deprivation (which, in turn, is frequently blamed on them and their deprived communities), but in an entirely unexpected direction. It's unexpected because it used to be the default setting of the Establishment and the police that the problem lay entirely with Afro-Caribbean immigrants and their descendants, and the Asians would keep quiet and work hard in their corner shops. I vividly remember the shock that greeted the Southall Riots of 1979 when the Asian population finally kicked back against the racist provocations of the National Front. It was shocking because the Asians simply weren't meant to behave like that.

Although I hardly dare say it, knowing the nature of the response I'll get, you could say exactly the same thing about the second generation of East European Jewish immigrants in the early part of the last century. Their parents kept quiet too, kept themselves to themselves and sought invisibility in the midst of an unwelcoming and hostile nation, and tended to live in detached communities of their own in the poorest part of town. Unsurprisingly, a lot of that second generation, showing the same kind of contempt for both their parents and their parents' choice of country, formed the backbone of the British Communist Party whose aim, lest we forget, was the violent overthrow of the British state and the establishment of a totalitarian dictatorship. Of course this involved a tiny minority of the Jewish community, but the Communist Party repaid their loyalty and were practically alone in giving them the sense of pride and purpose to stand up to the racism, deprivation and victimisation that assailed them from all sides. I'd argue that that, put simply, explains the attraction of Islamism to many young Muslims today, although I'd add the rider that I believe that the imposition of Sharia Law in this country is even less likely than Britain joining the Comintern in the 1930s.

The same factors motivate poor, terrified young black men to wander the streets near where I live in South London clutching handguns, to comfort themselves with the illusion of power and, therefore, control of a world over which they have the least control of anyone you care to think of.

The all-pervading revenge fantasy is universally alluring, most of all to the least powerful. We've already observed it in operation in the gibberish of the Book of Revelation, and also in Marxism. It's a kind of manic chutzpah, and was probably best articulated in Obi-Wan Kenobi's heart-warming defiance of Darth Vader during their last fight, halfway through the first Star Wars movie: 'If you kill me now, Darth, I'll become more powerful than you can begin to imagine!'

So, while it's obviously a tactic of militant political Islam, through its plots and atrocities, to provoke Western governments into further harrying and repression of those nations' already socially and economically beleaguered Muslim citizens in the hope of fomenting a general Muslim uprising, it strikes me as a kind of madness for clever journalists and cynical politicians to do half the job for them. If some poor and mostly powerless, often young and misguided people think they've found a way of evening up the equation between themselves and us by masquerading as our worst nightmare, demonising all Muslims because we fear and loathe the actions and attitudes of a small but noisy and rancorous section of Islam only helps them achieve their goal. We might imagine that we can shame them into silence by portraying them as demons, but the whole point of demons is that they're meant to be frightening.

More important, demons aren't human either.

Even if we find ourselves confronted by a group of people

we don't much like and we don't understand, a more nuanced response is required than just condemning everything about them out of hand. Personally, as a middle-aged white middle-class male I feel extremely uncomfortable when I see a woman walking down the street with her head covered by a black sack. I also know that wearing the veil is non-Qur'anic, inherently misogynistic and is further proof of many Muslims' lamentable abrogation of their own responsibilities when they justify it either because it's God's will, or because Muslim men claim that seeing the hair of any other woman apart from their wife would instantly transform them into slavering beasts driven solely by lust. When I hear comments like that I'm inclined to think that they should really try to get a grip. And I don't give a toss about cultural integrity if it involves shrouding women who don't want to be shrouded.

But how should I respond to women who want to wear the veil? Should I point out to them that they are fundamentally misguided? Yes I should, if I get the opportunity and I'm feeling rude enough. But what if they fail to be won over by my empowering arguments? Are we really proposing, as Jack Straw did recently when he said he couldn't hear his veiled Muslim constituents properly, that we target probably the poorest and least powerful group of people in British society and compel them to respond to my discomfort or his partial deafness?[30] And how do we achieve it? By pulling off women's veils in the streets? That way we become exactly the same as the police of the Ministry for the Promotion of Virtue and the Suppression of

---

[30] Straw never mentioned at the time that part of his problem in hearing his veiled constituents is that he depends, at least partially, on lip-reading as he was deafened in one ear when an IRA bomb exploded at the Old Bailey when he was still practising as a barrister. You'll observe the ironies of the casualty of one religionised conflict helping to fuel another one.

Vice in Tehran after the Islamic Revolution, who scrubbed lipstick from the faces of women with sandpaper.

*

It's often claimed by religionists that their faith has inspired them to create some of the greatest works of art known to man. Some more severe secularists have countered this by saying that that was all just a complete waste of time and money. Personally, I'd argue that Chartres Cathedral or Bach's *St Matthew Passion* are extraordinary monuments to man's ingenuity, and I don't really care if Chartres Cathedral or the Hagia Sophia or the Taj Mahal or Angkor Wat were originally built either to propitiate mythical gods or cow congregations or wider communities into awe at either the temporal power of the elite who had them built or the spiritual might of the gods to whom they were dedicated. (Nor do I care that St Pancras Station was built to awe railway passengers into increasing the profits for the capitalist gangsters who built it, or that Tate Modern has been adapted to cow us into a higher reverence for Art.) But I'd also argue that right up there with Chartres and the *St Matthew Passion* in the great by-products of religion is the Jewish joke.[31]

The Jewish joke is a truly beautiful thing, and works on so many different levels that I can't even begin to list them here. Its evolution is partly a result of the experiences of the Jewish

[31] My favourite example of the genre which is also one of the best jokes ever because of its layers of meaning, goes like this: two men are at a party in Golders Green, and the first bloke says to the other, 'Are you Jewish?' 'No,' says the other guy, so the first man says 'Are you sure you're not Jewish?' and the second man says, 'Honestly, I'm not Jewish' and then the first man says, 'Are you absolutely sure that you're not Jewish?' and the second man answers, 'Look, for the last time, I am not Jewish!' so the first man says, 'Funny. You don't look Jewish.'

diaspora, and partly an aspect of Judaism itself. Unlike its ungrateful monotheistic offspring Christianity and Islam, in my understanding of it Judaism is much more comfortable with the idea of humankind's relationship with God as a covenant – quite literally, a 'contract' – between equal parties. A lot of the history of Jewish theology is about rows with God, showing that it has a lot in common with Hellenic polytheism, whose devotees constantly complained about how completely bloody *unreasonably* the gods were behaving. This is in marked contrast to the abject subservience to God and his, her, its or their all-encompassing love that you tend to find in many parts of Christianity or Islam. Like most rows, humour plays its part on both sides, and it's often humour of the cruellest kind. The Book of Job, for instance, is more about happy slapping than the comforts of happy-clappy religion.[32]

I've already stated that I believe that humour is a hard-wired survival tool which is used in all sorts of different ways to achieve different ends. It can be used defensively or aggressively, to defuse dangerous situations or to exacerbate them, to give comfort or cause offence. Like many other

[32] In his wartime diaries, the Catholic writer Evelyn Waugh describes his time as an intelligence officer in Yugoslavia, where he and his colleagues Bob Laycock and Randolph Churchill, Prime Minister Winston Churchill's son, were meant to be liaising with Tito's partisans, but Tito would have nothing to do with them because Waugh, as a joke, had started a rumour that Tito was really a woman. This left the three of them with nothing to do, stuck in their tents in the middle of a rain-sodden field in the middle of Bosnia, so to pass the time (and to shut him up) Waugh bet Churchill that he couldn't read the Bible from cover to cover, as one of Waugh's nannies used to do, it being the only book she ever read. Churchill accepted the bet, and for a few days Waugh and Laycock finally got a bit of peace and quiet until Churchill burst into their tent, slamming his bible shut halfway through the Second Book of Kings with the memorable riposte, 'Jesus Christ! God really is a shit, isn't he?' After the war, when Churchill had a benign tumour surgically excised, Waugh observed 'I hear that Randolph's had the only non-malignant part of him removed.'

constructs of the human mind, humour exactly parallels
religion in its practical applications. Anyone can use it as a
weapon in any way they choose or are able. That's the
reason why I've deliberately written large parts of this book
in the flippant, ironic or even sarcastic way that I have.

In early 2006 we saw humour used as a weapon once
more in the frankly ridiculous row over the cartoons of the
Prophet Mohammed published in the Danish newspaper
Jyllands-Posten. It was ridiculous in part because many
people, on both sides of the barricades, behaved as stupidly
as it's possible to imagine.

As a cartoonist, I understand exactly how cartoons work.
As a subset of humour, they are exclusively knocking copy:
whether it's two blokes on a desert island or a cartoon of
George Bush eating a baby, basically they're a kind of non-
mystical voodoo, the purpose of which is to do damage to
your victim at a distance with a sharp object, in this case a
pen or pencil. It was highly disingenuous, therefore, for
defenders of *Jyllands-Posten*'s stance to claim that publish-
ing the cartoons was just a bit of fun, and thereafter to use
the highly effective yet utterly bogus tactic of crying 'Can't
you take a joke?' This becomes particularly obvious when
you consider the domestic Danish context in which the
cartoons were published, which was as part of a right-wing
newspaper's ongoing campaign against immigration.
Moreover, the cartoons were a provocation aimed at a poor,
powerless, beleaguered and probably frightened minority
within Denmark, a lot of whom doubtless clean *Jyllands-
Posten*'s offices and toilets and empty their bins.

As a political satirist, the acid test for my satire is H. L.
Mencken's definition of the purpose of journalism, which
will do for satire just as well: afflict the comfortable and
comfort the afflicted. In other words, only attack people
more powerful than you are, otherwise what you do ceases
to be satire, just like a cartoon that isn't knocking copy

instantly becomes just an illustration, in that strange counter-transubstantiation that we may not be able exactly to explain, but which we all understand. This is because the cartoon stops being funny, and when satire attacks the powerless it becomes nothing more than bullying.

In commissioning the cartoons, *Jyllands-Posten* failed the Mencken test, even though some of the cartoonists (who were paid about seventy quid each) double-bluffed the editors by producing cartoons attacking the paper for attacking Muslims.

However, the reaction by some Danish mullahs, just as right wing in their own way as the editors of *Jyllands-Posten*, passed the Mencken test with flying colours. As they hawked the cartoons round the courts of Middle Eastern despots, all they were really trying to do was increase their own power and influence. Thus, in my eyes as a satirist, the equation tipped against them. These were powerful men seeking to extend their power, and in order to do so added three further images to the ten cartoons which were originally published. One of these was of a Muslim at prayer being sodomised by a dog, and although its provenance is still unclear, there's every possibility that the mullahs commissioned it themselves. But, like many, many other special interest groups – like the Zionists who called me an anti-semite (and worse), or many other groups who've filled my email inbox with their bile – the Danish mullahs used taking offence as an offensive weapon of their own, adding their own exquisite special dimension with the customary death threats. This was on top of the government in Riyadh sponsoring demonstrations, in a country where I think you'll find spontaneous demonstrations of any kind are pretty few and far between, while the Syrian government bussed their own thugs into Beirut to burn down the Danish legation, using the cartoons as a pretext to flex their geopolitical muscles as part of their own, quite unrelated agenda in the region.[33] Meanwhile, throughout the Islamic world local mullahs retrenched and sought to expand their own political power by fomenting their congregations into a frenzy of pious outrage, while in London stupid young men dressed up as suicide bombers and bellowed 'Freedom of speech! Go to hell!' in the streets. One of them was thereafter forced to apologise on TV, flanked by his dad and his imam, both of whom he was probably trying to piss off in the first place, like many stupid young men, while some of his chums went to prison for inciting murder.

The only real result of any importance in all this nonsense was that dozens and dozens of Muslims were shot dead in their own Muslim countries by Muslim policemen because they'd rioted to further the political ambitions of Muslim clerics. I worked out long ago that humour is a serious business, but the obscene ironies involved here once more prove that reality will always outstrip satire. In other words, you couldn't make it up. Also, with the best or worst will in the world, you couldn't make up the almost unbelievable political ineptitude of the many, often self-appointed spokesmen for Islam. It's true that stirring up a global row about the Danish cartoons achieved a short-term result in using the catch-all tactic of taking offence, but the long-term consequence was that they made their great world religion look like nothing more than the petulant child in the playground who thumps you for simply looking at them. In short, they made themselves far more of a laughing stock than a few daft drawings ever could.

Nor, indeed, could you make up the equally ridiculous response of many Europeans who backed themselves

[33] I appeared on a discussion programme on one of Channel 4's subsidiary channels at the time, and suggested that our response should be to burn down the Syrian embassy in London, for a laugh, and then boycott Saudi oil, for our own good as well as theirs and the planet's. Luckily no one was watching.

further and further into the most extreme corner they could find, claiming the paramountcy of freedom of expression over absolutely everything else, and bugger the consequences. I encountered this attitude for myself a few months later when I went to the British Academy to the launch of a book for which I'd designed the cover. To my dismay, I quickly realised that the launch wasn't just the usual warm white wine and Twiglets affair I'd been hoping for, but included a debate on the state of the media chaired by the ex-Communist journalist John Lloyd. Lloyd is another of those pro-war lefties or ex-lefties, whom I prefer to call neo-tankies,[34] who've dragged their Manichean mindset from the Cold War and insist on seeing the final battle between good and evil just round the next corner. He finished the meeting with a digression, saying that it was an unforgivable scandal that the Mohammed cartoons were not republished by every newspaper in Britain. After he'd closed the debate, although the warm white wine was beckoning, I went up to take issue with him, to suggest that his approach was slightly unnuanced. He responded with fury, getting crosser and crosser as he asserted that freedom of expression was more important than absolutely everything else. And I'm afraid that I failed to respond to his invitation as I should have done, and therefore failed to exercise my right to complete, unfettered freedom of

[34] I came up with this word to describe Lloyd, Hitchens, Aaronovitch and the rest of them in an article I wrote for *Tribune* about my friend Nick Cohen's book *What's Left?* It honours the pro-war ex-left's origins by acknowledging the **neo**conservatives, that bunch of ex-Trots who believe in the violent export of democracy throughout the world on the back of the US military-industrial complex, and the **tankies**, the diehards of the old British Communist Party who supported Stalin or Moscow's line at every turn, above and beyond accepting unquestioningly Soviet tanks trundling through Budapest or into Czechoslovakia in the violent suppression of the Hungarian Uprising of 1956 and the Prague Spring of 1968.

expression by yelling at him, 'Then why don't you just fuck off, you ugly Scottish cunt?'

It's obvious to me that free expression is no more the highest principle than demanding that you be protected from anything and everything that you might choose to be offended by. I'm deeply offended by people believing in God, but realistically I don't expect billions of people to cry with one voice 'We're really sorry, Martin; we'll stop it right away.' As to freedom of expression, it's contingent on many other things, and so-called political correctness is merely the latest, necessarily blunt instrument to attempt to make us behave reasonably well in company.

That's actually the point. There is a clear division between public and private discourse, and the reasons why humour, or satire, or cartoons, or indeed swearing work, and why we use them, is because they transgress those boundaries when we need to do so to our advantage. Although the mono-theistic religions all contain the tendency towards being both monopolistic and monolithic, in practice they're constantly firefighting against the realities on the ground of everyone constantly breaking the taboos they've created. Those realities are you and me, beings infinitely more complicated in our behaviour, predilections and motiv-ations than can be accommodated within their narrow systems. That's one reason why I'm an atheist. But I'm many other things as well, and my political scepticism – the thing that made me a satirist – arises from my recognition of the same tendency to simplify us to fit many other templates as well. I referred to this earlier when I described how social and biological scientists look at us as data, capitalists and advertisers look at us as units of production or consump-tion, and so on. But we're better than that; much, much better, because we're infinitely if infuriatingly more compli-cated in our wonderful, magnificent human diversity.

Maybe it's significant that it took an Anglican clergyman

to sum it up best of all, in one of the most genuinely human sentences ever written. I make no apology for repeating the passage from Jonathan Swift's 'Digression on Madness' in *A Tale of a Tub* with which I've prefaced this book, because it's so important it should probably be tattooed on the forehead of every priest, politician, scientist and advertising manager on Earth: 'For what man in the natural state or course of thinking, did ever conceive it in his power to reduce the notions of all mankind exactly to the same length, and breadth, and height as his own?'

But it's another Anglican clergyman who can help us out of some more immediate problems. The Red Queen in Lewis Carroll's *Through the Looking-Glass* famously said, 'Why, sometimes I've believed as many as six impossible things before breakfast.' And we're capable of doing just the same. It may not display consistency, but if we'd done that we'd still be amoebae. But still, if your political bent is not totalitarian, or you're not blinded by Manicheanism or substitute racism, in this context you should have no problem whatsoever in sympathising, or maybe even empathising, with poor and beleaguered Muslims and their families while still deploring the narrowness and short- sightedness of their self-selected spokesmen, while simultaneously supporting the efforts of Muslims in Muslim countries using whatever methods they can to free themselves of the corrupt and incompetent despots who rule them, even if you deplore the wider implications of the political Islamism they resort to, while at exactly the same time utterly deploring the crass interventions of Western powers to bolster those despots, but also actively supporting, advocating and defending the Western way of life to the death.

Some people would say that thinking like that is non-sensical, or at least illogical. I'd say it's human, and you can believe those six impossible, or at least contradictory things, before or after breakfast, precisely because you are human.

That's the reason why, although I'm an atheist, and also a humanist (while not necessarily being a Humanist), I'm not a rationalist. This is because humans aren't entirely rational, and nor should we be. Nor, I suspect, would many of us wish us to be.

Our species' myths and legends, as well as subsequent literatures for adults and children, are crammed full of stories about emotion overcoming rationality; of impetuosity, inspired by love, romance or, for that matter, martyrdom, overcoming cold, hard logic. That's why we prefer stories like those to precise and exacting factual descriptions of accountants poring over a spreadsheet. Those stories are also populated by gods, demons, fairies, elves, ghosts, goblins and, over and over again, talking animals. We bring up our children with teddy bears and comfort blankets, and we fill their minds and imaginations from almost the moment they're born with the idea of anthropomorphic animals.

However, just in case you didn't realise it, this, like Santa Claus and the Tooth Fairy, is a lie.[35] It's a lie because animals can't talk, and the fact that they can't talk is what makes us so uniquely different from them, or so we're told.

Earlier on I mentioned the lecture I attended at London

[35] During the period of years when our children, born twenty months apart, lost their milk teeth, I got a great deal of self-indulgent pleasure from writing them long letters in immaculate copperplate purporting to be from the Tooth Fairy. These would detail her various adventures

Zoo given by the atheist geneticist Steve Jones. Afterwards,
I went up to him and said that I'd thoroughly enjoyed the
lecture, but wondered if it had occurred to him that by
talking up the qualitative difference that he'd argued meant
that humans weren't animals he'd exposed a chink in his
atheist armour, through which some people might try to
inject God. He gave me a look of pure loathing, but chose
not to make any further comment. That said, a few weeks
earlier Jones did agree to make some comments about the
nature of good and evil, and when asked for an example of
evil had cited religionists, because they lie to children. I've
already given you my definition of evil, which I believe is
defined by the degree to which you consider, or neglect to
consider, the consequences of your actions on other people.
In the swirling maelstrom in which we make snap judgements to affect our behaviour, I suspect that always telling
the truth, inasmuch as we can ever hope to know what it is,
would probably hobble us into complete non-functionality.

But I still sort of agree with him. There are obviously
degrees of lying, and terrifying little children into mute and
unquestioning obedience by threatening them with terrible
but entirely unknowable and unverifiable consequences
after they're dead is definitely down the bad end of the
scale. I also agree with him in his avowed atheism, otherwise I wouldn't have written this book and further
burdened both you and the remainder bins.

in negotiating her way to their pillows to get the tooth, how much it
would be worth on the international tooth market, how walrus tusks
were performing badly against a basket of narwhal horns and
vampires' fangs, and so on. On one occasion, when our daughter
refused to go to sleep, we even balanced the quid bit she was getting
for the tooth (we live in inflationary times, toothwise) on the back of
Sybil the cat and pushed her into Rose's room first thing the following
morning. I hope this admission doesn't add to the charge sheet against
me for being evil for lying to my children, or unduly traumatise them
now they've discovered the Truth.

Yet I hope I've achieved something different from previous books in this now crowded genre. I've presented you with my analysis of how and why I think religions have evolved, and why many of us invest so much of our energy and faith in them. According to the empirical principles of some of my scientifically trained co-writers, analysis and explanation is, or should be, value neutral, although often it isn't. I'll leave it up to you to decide whether my case is compelling or otherwise. But the question then inevitably arises: what do we do next?

Professor Dawkins and Christopher Hitchens analysed religion too, and on the weight of the evidence decided it was a bad thing. I think that by and large it's a bad thing too, but for slightly different reasons. I should also admit that I've been misleading you by talking about 'religion', although given the fact that I've been trying to present you with an insanely ambitious overview, you might be generous enough to forgive me. I should, of course, have been talking about 'religions'.

I wrote earlier that the Archbishop of Canterbury is, to all intents and purposes, indistinguishable from a slug. This is true, in the broadest sense of both creatures. Both are made of matter, both are alive and both exist in Time. Yet for everyday purposes it's probably more expedient to recognise their differences in order to avoid unnecessary confusion, and accept that one of them exudes slimy mucus to aid its locomotion through its life and decimates your prize cabbages while the other one has a bushy beard and eyebrows and wears a frock. To claim that both lack a backbone, allowing them to wriggle themselves into all sorts of weird shapes, is just another cheap satirical point which we should probably ignore. It's the recognition of their differences which allows us to respond to each of them differently, by choosing maybe to sprinkle one with salt and hurl a cushion across the room when we see the other one on the telly. Or maybe just ignore both, and leave them to get on with whatever it is they do. The same applies to religions.

We know that religions are different from each other. That's why they fight. But in addition to my suggestion that you can identify the origins and the success of many religions in politics, I don't think (although I also don't know) that therein lies the origin of all religion.

It's more likely that, like so much else, religion began as another expedient protocol for helping us navigate our way through life, and to help us order and control our lives. If there ever was a founding religion, an ur-theology from which all other religions grew, then it seems obvious to me that you can see it in the animist religions of so-called 'primitive' peoples, rather than in later manifestations of the phenomenon, like monotheism. And animism makes a great deal of sense: it helps you locate yourself not just in space, by reinforcing through an imposed sense of the sacred the landmarks of your environment, but in Time as well, through the veneration of your ancestors.

Time, again, is a defining factor. Earlier, I described two possible perceptions of Time, the scientific/materialist idea of Progress and the theological/eschatological concept of progress towards material catastrophe, followed by spiritual perfection. There are, of course, many ways of looking at Time, and these two both look at it backwards. From our point of view as humans, it's almost inevitable that we see everything existing in Time in a confused way, mixing up subjective and objective. We tend, for instance, to see things that have happened most recently as 'new' and 'fresh', and the longer ago something happened, the older and staler it becomes. Because of the way we view ourselves in Time (for more reasons than I can properly address here), we're not predisposed to recognise that, with equal validity, the oldest things that happened were originally the freshest, and the latest are merely their latest and stalest manifestations. Looked at this way, Time is more about the process of entropy and decay than it is about Progress.

We all half-recognise this, but at the same time fail to accept its implications, although with a human phenomenon like religion, it seems to me that it's particularly important that we should. There is a generally accepted belief, at least among its adherents, that the latest manifestation of a religious sensibility is the best, because it's undergone a process of refinement and improvement – thus Christianity is 'better' than Judaism, then after that Islam is 'better' than Christianity, Protestantism 'better' than Catholicism and so on. All of them are better than any of the religions that preceded them, all the way back to 'primitive' animism. Within that dynamic, a simpler, purer past is also constantly invoked, although the implications of that are seldom taken to their obvious conclusion: that animism is the purest form of religion, and that everything that has grown from it is merely evidence of decay, which happens inevitably because religion, like everything else we experience, exists within Time.

When Europeans first arrived in Australia, among the first humans they encountered were a tribe of hunter-gatherers living around what the invaders named Botany Bay. We now know they'd been there for about 40,000 years, without showing any signs of material progress whatsoever. Instead, they lived lives of almost idyllic ease, spending only a couple of hours a day gathering from the seashore all they required for a reasonably comfortable existence. Not only was this the opposite of the atheist philosopher Thomas Hobbes' description of the life of the 'savage' as 'nasty, brutish and short', but was tellingly described by Robert Hughes in his history of the Australian penal settlements, *The Fatal Shore*. Hughes added that, if a native Australian was suddenly transported to eighteenth-century London, he or she would have looked in horror at the filth, deprivation and degradation of life and exclaimed 'So this is your Third World!'

Because their lives were so comparatively easy, and because they didn't bother themselves with ideas of progress or improvement, these people had little else to do during those forty millennia except sit around telling each other stories. But the consequence was that after thousands and thousands of years, these stories became legends, then myths, then a theology, and their descendants ended up with the most complex taboo system known to anthropology.

The point of telling you this is to show the importance of factoring in Time to the rest of the equation of human existence, and see how it operates. Time rots. It also hardens and withers and fossilises. If you accept animism as the ur-religion, its expedient protocols have been concreted into absolute certainties while religion, as a human construct, has aged. Its arteries have become sclerotic, lesions have split and cross-hatched it, tumours have filled its internal organs and blemished its skin. In short, from its origins in unknowably distant time religion may have appeared to have undergone refinement, improvement and renewal, but in truth it is a man-made monument to the inescapable power of decay. And this is true particularly of the so-called Religions of the Book, where protocols thousands of years old are fossilised through written words into a terrible, immovable certainty, however inappropriate or downright dangerous they become in changed circumstances. That's why the political programmes of these political religions are so barren and unattractive, and have atrophied into being almost exclusively about personal behaviour. It's because their manifestos are so hopelessly out of date that they're not equipped to deal with more recent contingencies.[36]

However, we have to deal with what we've got. So, irrespective of how we ended up where we now are in the evolution of religion into its infinite variety, it's still important to recognise that this variety exists. So we have religions of war and religions of peace, religions of love and hate, and many which are all four simultaneously. We also have materialist religions, as well as extremely anti-materialist ones; tolerant and intolerant religions; deeply intellectual and proudly anti-intellectual religions, and again these aspects often co-exist within the same religion. There are also lackey religions who grovel before kings, and emancipating religions which heroically oppose and seek to thwart all the trappings and corruptions of worldy power. And, of course, there are religions which are pure racketeering.[37] This diversity perfectly mirrors the diversity within us and to all intents and purposes is simply another manifestation of human diversity. That's why we should recognise that there's a world of difference between a Quaker, actively involved in the Peace Movement and doing genuine good for other people, and Osama Bin Laden's murderous and deranged heretical branch of a branch of a branch of Islam.

[36] Literacy has a lot to answer for, including, of course, this book.
[37] You can fill in the names of the cult of your choice, and across the board. The unjustly neglected *Playboy* cartoonist B. Kliban summed it up rather neatly in a cartoon of the Pope, surrounded by his cardinals, saying 'Church attendance is down, boys. Let's split the money and head for the coast!' More germanely to my wider thesis, another of his cartoons shows a dog in a church, kneeling in prayer before an altar, while behind him a priest is pointing to the door and saying 'You! Out!' His best cartoon deals with everything: it shows a theatre with a huge queue outside. In enormous letters on the front of the theatre are the words 'Go Fuck Yourself!' The cartoon is captioned 'The Only Show in Town'.

In fact, this proliferation of faith suggests to me the lack of God just as much as the proliferation of life makes many people believe that God must exist. Because the diversity within religion implies either incompetence, untidiness, impotence or non-existence in an omniscient, omnipotent creator, as omniscience and omnipotence don't really fit in with the first three observable qualities of God I've plumbed for the fourth. But if you focus in more closely, even though they may share the same dicta, I think there's also a difference between a vicious, dirty-minded priest who bullies children or browbeats adults into a very narrow range of human behaviour and a little old lady who arranges the flowers in his church. But even when religionists hold almost identical views, it's significant that there will still be other things which separate them, like right wing, reactionary, homophobic American Christian fundamentalists who believe in family values,[38] and right wing, reactionary, homophobic Iranian

---

[38] 'Family values', like 'morality', are something else I'm instantly suspicious of whenever they're invoked, because they invariably involve the narrowest possible definition of the family. But even though cynical politicians frequently declare the family to be the basic unit of society the fact is that the social unit for our kind of primate is the group or tribe. The family unit is too small and too claustrophobic, which is why many families are often riven by vicious hatreds and jealousies, as shown in the biblical story of Cain and Abel. You can see this in metaphorical families too, like the Umma or Brotherhood of all Muslims where, like a lot of brothers, throughout the Muslim world Shias and Sunnis can't wait to kill each other. Nor should we forget metaphorical families within religion and all those desexed Holy Fathers, barren Mothers Superior, sexless Brothers and Sisters and us as the suffering little children, expected to be seen in church but not heard, except when we sing unquestioning praise or confess to our congenital wickedness. Still, whether it's Holy Families or Royal Families, the priests and politicians keep peddling the traditional nuclear family, probably because it's the largest social unit they can ever possibly hope to control. As to that popular political mantra about 'hard-working families', it shouldn't be forgotten that idle singletons have a vote too.

Muslim fundamentalists, who hate each other for almost purely geopolitical reasons.

And yet the message I get from Dawkins and Hitchens is that the Quaker and the old lady are as complicit in the infamies and inexactitudes of religion as Bin Laden, the priest or the American or Iranian fundamentalists. It's like the common secularist taunt that religion is just a comfort blanket for the infantile or the inadequate. This may indeed be true, but the thing about a comfort blanket is that it comforts you. And anyway, what kind of schmuck takes a comfort blanket from a child, at the same time telling them that they're wrong, and evil too?

Essentially, I feel a lot of our leading Humanists ought to try to be a bit more human. There's a kind of terrible Gradgrindism to a lot of contemporary anti-religious thinking, and it brings to mind the definitions of the two sides in the English Civil Wars in W. C. Sellar's and R. J. Yeatman's classic absurdist history of Britain *1066 and All That*. Dawkins is right in his analysis, and so is Hitchens. And yet like Sellar's and Yeatman's Roundheads they are Right but Repulsive. Meanwhile, you have to concede that a lot of religion, in all its idiocies and illogicalities, is often Wrong but Wromantic.

The political contingencies that faced the world after the murderous atrocities wrought in Manhattan on 11 September 2001 led a lot of people to conclude that religion was the root of the problem. In *The God Delusion* Dawkins writes that those attacks would not have taken place, and all those people wouldn't have died, if religion didn't exist in the first place. I believe that to be a profoundly mistaken and dangerous analysis. That's why I've sought to demonstrate the political nature of most religion, and how religion is not just often an indivisible dimension of politics, but just as likely to be used as a tactic as part of

wider political struggles. Previous generations of more
purely political fanatics may have been less ruthless, but
they were just as prepared to die for their cause, with or
without the promise of paradise and those seventy-two
virgins. In fact, ridiculing suicide bombers by highlighting
this admittedly ridiculous aspect of their possible motivations is probably counterproductive. I'm all for laughing
Al Qaeda's kind of kite-banning, music-banning, beard-
growing, but also women-hating and gay-killing political
Islam back into the dustbin of history where it belongs, but
it seems to me more sensible to place it within the political
context of the thousands of different dialectical struggles
for power and control, and justice as well, which have
flowed throughout the whole of human history with no
sign of any final or lasting synthesis. To put it bluntly,
saying that potential suicide bombers should stop it
because of the unlikelihood of that promised ectoplasmic
shag after they've blown themselves to bits won't cancel
out the political realities they suffer under Israeli or
American occupation (or under many Arab or Muslim
governments), or the intensity of the rage they feel because
of their powerlessness, and the serial humiliations they
consider their culture has endured, even if a lot of that is the
fault of the culture itself. Once more, these are political
struggles, should be accepted as such and responded to
accordingly, depending on your political stance. And if you
think I'm being altogether too understanding, remember
that it's essential to explain the world before you can have
any hope of changing it.

But to repeat the question, what *do* we do next? It's
tempting, in the face of all the cruelty and absurdity
associated with religion, just to make a bonfire of the
inanities and the insanities and be done with it. Except that
it won't work. Arguing against religionists on the grounds

of logic or scientific provability again misses the point entirely. One of the main attractions of religion is that it *isn't* logical, that it appeals to that part of us based in our imagination, that actually relishes the irrational.

In the infinity of different factors that affect our lives, this can take you anywhere. When I was at university I knew two young men, one a student in London, the other studying law in Cambridge, both of whom I happened to meet over the course of the same weekend. When I asked each of them how he was, both replied that they had been miserable because they'd both recently been dumped by their girlfriends. But both of them were now beginning to feel a lot better because the Cambridge student had found God and joined his college's Evangelical Christian Group, while the London student had found Trotsky and joined the Socialist Workers Party. And who can blame them? Both groups offered a totalitarian sense of certainty and purpose in a confused and troubled world, although the precepts of both were and are equally risible. My two friends, in identical ways but in different directions, had compensated for the pains they'd suffered thanks to the illogicalities of love with other, more structured irrationalities.

It's not just irrationality that's attractive. Bone-headed anti-intellectualism has always been as tempting to aspirant intellectuals as to anyone else, as is drinking yourself into idiocy. That (the anti-intellectualism, not the drinking) applies to the young British Asian men and women who fall for the kinds of totalitarian Islam currently being peddled on some of our university campuses, but it also goes across the board. Again when I was a student, two Christians, who I knew to be intelligent, pretty rational and funny, thought they'd finally skewered my atheism by asking me, with smiling intensity, 'But who moved the stone?' I'm afraid I

answered, 'Who fucking cares?'[39] Irrespective of my foul
mouth, it was still a question of mind-numbing banality,
although it obviously did the trick for them.

Even among the avowedly intellectual, the irrational is
still a lure. Someone else I knew at the time was a highly
intelligent semi-pagan hippy English student who'd started
reading St Thomas Aquinas and was, he claimed, captivated
by Aquinas' intellectual arguments. If I could be bothered to
read them, I'd probably conclude that they were as
intellectually rigorous as a tabernacle made of yogurt if
you're not inclined to make the initial leap of faith into faith.
But, as he told me later, he also discovered that Aquinas was
believed by his contemporaries to be able to levitate
(Hitchens alludes to this with contempt in *God Is Not Great*)
while at the same time being rumoured to be *the fattest man
in Europe*. That, for my erstwhile pagan hippy friend, was
the clincher, and we should never underestimate either the
joy we feel at the daring of the improbable or the attraction
of the whimsical, which is just the pale end of the spectrum
of irrationality.

For the record, this man is now an ordained Anglican

---

[39] When I originally gave the talk on which this book is based in that
upper room in Catford, one of my audience was a quiet, bespectacled
man in early middle age, who'd listened quietly and politely to what
I had to say. After I'd finished, he asked a question, saying he had to
take issue with my comment about who moved the stone from
Christ's tomb, misquoting me by saying I'd said, 'Who cares?' The
point was, he went on, that the resurrection of Our Lord Jesus Christ
was the most important event in the whole of history, and he had
personal experience of life after death. Whether or not he'd
deliberately chosen to be my Judas I don't know, although you can't
help but admire someone who is willing to sit in a rough pub in
Catford on a March night simply in order to get his point across to
people who profoundly disagreed with him. Be that as it may,
another member of the audience then said, 'So does that mean you're
alive or dead?'

vicar, who has been on a decades-long mission to the Hell's
Angels of East Anglia to whom he ministers on his motorbike, which you can see as either ridiculous or rather
endearing. The last time I met him, at a college reunion
several years ago, he reminded me that I'd gone a couple of
times to some church services, out of politeness when asked
to, and in order better to understand the enemy. 'Yes,' he
sighed. 'We thought we'd got you then.' At which point he
stopped being endearing and became suddenly rather
sinister instead.

But despite his terrible compulsion to keep on recruiting
and make me the same length and height and breadth as him,
we ought to give my born-again Thomist chum some credit
for wholeheartedly embracing the irrational and sticking
with it, and also accepting its potency and importance in his
life and the lives of others.

Indeed, the English understand, or at least manifest, the
coexistence of rationality and irrationality better than many.
John Locke, whose political philosophy largely underwrote
the Glorious Revolution of 1688, can also claim to be one of
the founding fathers of the brand of English empiricism that
flowered in the Enlightenment and in its turn further
diminished the power of religion. However, if you count
both the Industrial Revolution and the British Empire as
offspring of both the Enlightenment and 1688, these were
also largely the products of empiricism working in relative
harmony with Evangelical Christianity and capitalism,
which I've already suggested is an entirely irrational
construct, based as it is on an unverifiable faith in profits
through prophecy.

This coexistence goes further. The famous debate on
evolution at the British Association meeting in Oxford in
1860s where 'Darwin's bulldog' Thomas Henry Huxley
slugged it out with Bishop Samuel Wilberforce, is seen by
many as the first great salvo in the battle between

Darwinism and religion.[40] Nonetheless, both sides thought they'd won the debate, both sides enjoyed themselves enormously and both sides went off for a very jolly dinner together afterwards. More than that, a week later Huxley and Wilberforce were both back working together on the Gardens Committee at London Zoo, happily collaborating on important decisions concerning the husbandry of eland. What this demonstrates is that neither Huxley nor Wilberforce thought that their profound differences were paramount, to the point where they ceased to be friends.

After 1688, in tolerant, pluralist, quasi-democratic England it was inevitable (because it was built into the political settlement) that irrationality and rationality would coexist in society just as they coexist in all of us as individuals, albeit in constant conflict. But the conflict was part of the point. Swift, though a Tory and a fierce opponent of the Whig Revolution, epitomised the principles of that revolution in those lines about reducing everyone to the same length and height and breadth, but it is significant that he did so in a section of *A Tale of a Tub* titled 'A Digression on Madness'.

Throughout the eighteenth century, madness ran in parallel and in counterpoint to the English Enlightenment. Whether it's Hogarth's Rake going mad, or the (arguably hyper-empirical) absurdity of Sterne's *Tristram Shandy*, or the rise of The Gothick and Romanticism, empiricism never had a clear run at it, and the last two examples were specific reactions against all that reason and common sense. One of the legacies of this is that the English now venerate their

[40] Debating evolution in the light of the publication of Darwin's *On the Origin of Species*, Wilberforce, as a cheap joke, asked Huxley if he was descended from an ape on his mother's or his father's side of the family. Huxley counterployed by deliberately refusing to see the joke and replied that he'd rather be descended from an ape than from a man like Wilberforce who deliberately misused his great talents.

very own secular English mystic in the form of William
Blake. A strictly empirical response to Blake would
diagnose him, I believe correctly, as an obvious schizo-
phrenic whose visions of angels sitting in the trees on
Peckham Rye should more properly be described as
delusional hallucinations. But none of this invalidates the
power of his vision or the strength of his anti-rational
message, and I'm not alone in hoping beyond hope that on
that happy day when Harry Marten's English Republic is
restored, it will adopt Blake's 'Jerusalem' as its national
anthem (with words by a madman, music by a Guild
socialist and a profoundly religious sentiment).

Returning to Swift, we've already seen how one
eighteenth-century bishop didn't believe a word of
Gulliver's Travels. He was quite right not to, on strictly
empirical grounds, although to the point of absurdity. One
of the other weird yet wonderful things about the English
is that we're meant to be rational and empirical as well as
being notoriously emotionally repressed, and yet we're
globally celebrated for our novelists and our actors, both of
whom are, in the strictest sense of term, shamelessly
emotional and barefaced liars to boot. That, again, is to
take things to absurd degrees of rectitude, but in the
nineteenth century Swift suffered a worse fate than being
accused of lying: many people thought he was mad. This
was thanks to a rationalist misreading of the final book of
Gulliver's Travels, where Lemuel Gulliver visits the Land of
the Houyhnhnms, a race of noble horses who personified
(equified?) pure reason. Although his contemporaries got
the joke, later readers saw in this book a terrible kind of
misanthropy in Swift's portrayal of humans as the Yahoos,
bestial, apelike creatures of fathomless depravity
(although he was also pre-empting Darwin by 130 years).
But this is a fundamental misinterpretation of what Swift
was trying to say. The Houyhnhnms may be pure reason,

but the whole point of them is that they are not *human*, and neither is their perfection. Remember that this is satire: although Gulliver may admire the Houyhnhnms to the point where, on his return to England, he abandons his family to live in a stable, that doesn't mean that Swift shared the opinions of his creation. Rather than being misanthropic, once more Swift was being profoundly human in recognising through exaggeration the human flaws we all share. And Gulliver's departure from the Land of the Houyhnhnms, in a coracle made from the cured pelts of Yahoos, is as horrific in its ironic depiction of the inhumanity of the purely rational as was Swift's ironic suggestion in *A Modest Proposal* that the best solution for famine in Ireland was for the Irish to eat their children.

Then again, as I've often discovered in my professional career, irony has a depressing tendency to fall flat on its face as it trips over the far greater absurdities of real life. Of course, falling flat on your face is just another of the countless things we respond to by laughing, and laughter is also our common response to the absurd and the irrational, and it could be argued that all humour has its basis in helping us survive the inexplicable, including the irrational, and the mad are as much the object of our laughter as kings or priests or our next-door neighbour falling off their roof. After all, Swift was hoping to make us laugh, albeit darkly, at the absurdity and irrationality of pure reason as much as he was laughing at the Court of Queen Anne, transformed into the homunculi of the Empire of Lilliput.

In the case of the irrationality of religion, however, laughter isn't an option. In fact, because it's the obvious immediate response, laughing in the face of God, alleged miracles, hidden imams, hoped-for messiahs, virgins in paradise, bearded men in dresses, life after death and the rest of it is intolerable to all totalitarian religions, just as it was when the little boy laughed at the emperor's new clothes. That doesn't obviate the power of the allure of the irrational in religion for millions of people, even though religions dress their absurdity and irrationality in a deadly earnestness, which frequently turns to even deadlier fury when religionists insist that 'God is not mocked!'[41] But as the English socialist and atheist Edward Aveling used to say at the start of his lectures against religion: 'The Bible tells us that Jesus wept. But did he ever laugh?'[42]

*

Although I'm not accusing Richard Dawkins of promoting pure reason to the exclusion of everything else, the emphasis he places on the irrationality of religion and the rationality and reasonableness of its opponents is where his whole approach begins to break down. His brand of rational,

[41] This cuts every which way. Given the outraged response to a cartoon I recently drew of Richard Dawkins for an atheist magazine I work for, it's clear the categories are infinitely interchangeable in the following joke, which was originaly about feminists, but obviously now includes everybody who has an opinion about anything. Here we go, then: Q: How many atheists does it take to change a lightbulb? A: THAT ISN'T FUNNY! By the same token, how many religious fundamentalists does it take to change a lightbulb? None. They HATE the Enlightenment!

[42] Aveling (1849–1898) had a hard time of it. His first wife left him because she couldn't stand his atheism, and he lost his lecturing job at King's College London for the same reason. Then he was driven out of the National Secular Society because Charles Bradlaugh, the NSS's founder, couldn't stand Aveling's Marxism, and Marx's daughter Eleanor, his partner for many years, committed suicide while nursing him during his final bout of kidney failure because she couldn't stand his serial infidelity. Along the way he left the Social Democratic Federation to set up the Socialist League for the usual sectarian reasons, although no one from either organisation went to his funeral, four months after Eleanor's death, because by and large no one at all could stand him. The current author is an honorary associate of the National Secular Society.

unforgiving and, in its own way, totalitarian atheism, however consoling it may be to his fellow atheists and secularists,
is unlikely to mark the final death of religion.[43]

It's also worth pointing out that religion is by no
means alone in trading on irrationality in dangerous and
destructive ways.

I've just reminded you about the irrationality of capitalism, but add to that the madness of the housing market, or
all the other madnesses like the faith that economics must
be predicated on never-ending economic growth. Then
there's globalisation, the purchasing policies of British
supermarkets and cheap air travel, irrespective of the
environmental cost of our rapacious demand for a bargain.
Add to those the completely irrational way successive
British governments have grovelled to the born-again
Christian, monopolist and dynast Rupert Murdoch,
based entirely on their belief and fear in his apparent
omnipotence, even though he's actually more like the
Wizard of Oz than like God, although everyone's too
mesmerised and frightened by him to call his bluff.[44] Despite
the way elected politicians lickspittle to Murdoch, he is
himself one of the greatest lickspittles in history, always
prepared to kowtow to power whatever its shape or nature,
in order to make more money for himself. His shamelessness
in this regard is well documented, whether it's the
Communist Chinese or dropping the Tories as soon as it
became obvious that Tony Blair's New Labour would win
the 1997 British general election. However, this is where

[43] I once heard a story about Dawkins, which probably isn't true but
I'll repeat it anyway. He was visiting an art gallery in Florence, and
was heard to comment as he came out, 'But what's all this art *for*?'
[44] When his daughter Elizabeth and her husband Matthew Freud had
their first baby, Murdoch's ex-wife Anna was reported to have said:
'Poor little thing! Imagine being born with the genes of Sigmund
Freud *and* Rupert Murdoch!'

Murdoch shows his true genius, in exactly the same way as shamans have throughout history. His various media outlets support whoever's in power, or is likely to be, but in second-guessing a result he makes neurotic and paranoid politicians make it seem like he's produced it, and saying that It Was the *Sun* Wot Won the 1992 British general election is precisely the same as overawing your tribe into worship and subservience by correctly anticipating a solar eclipse.

Then there's advertising. There seems to me that an exquisite kind of madness has allowed the Industry of Lies more or less to destroy British television, and arguably large parts of the rest of our politics and culture as well, because of advertising's faith in the dream demographic of 18-24-year-olds, who must be pursued and propitiated at any cost not only with unbelievably crass programming but with ever more TV channels broadcasting endless garbage. This isn't because the dream demographic is *rich*, but because they're *gullible*, and therefore more likely to believe advertising's lies. This is something the Jesuits worked out centuries ago.

And, once again, there's the medical elite, who expend a lot of time and energy telling us what and what not to eat, drink and smoke, without ever appearing to address why we do those things, and the economic and social circumstances that both allow us and compel us to drive ourselves into an early grave. There are legion irrational and oppressive establishments worth kicking in addition to, or even instead of, religion. But I suppose it's always easiest to kick a man when he's down, and Oxford professors or journalists who enjoy the hospitality of State Department spooks, while enthusiastically embracing the first part, won't necessarily buy into the whole of that old anarchist war cry: 'Burn the churches! Smash the state!'

*

Dawkins prefaces *The God Delusion* with a dedication to the memory of his dead friend Douglas Adams, author of *The Hitchhiker's Guide to the Galaxy*, and with the following quotation: 'Isn't it enough to see that a garden is beautiful without having to believe that there are fairies at the bottom of it too?' The trouble with that laudable sentiment is that it leaves out the human element.

We're predisposed to populate everything around us with the creations of our imaginations as we project our empathy in all directions, second-guessing what's hidden in the shrubbery. Once we bother looking there, the 'rational' parts of our minds will inform us that there aren't in fact any fairies there at all, and so as usual we'll continue to navigate our way through our lives making judgement calls based on the evidence of our own eyes. But that first second-guess has already lodged in our brains, and diffuses out into our other thoughts, and we might still conclude that there really are fairies at the bottom of the garden simply because we like the idea. We like its unlikelihood; we like the notion of an alternative to the dull reality of our observable, mundane existence. Then we're charmed by the thought of the fairies; we might even laugh at the thought that the fairies are really there, and in so doing we release some endorphins into the biochemical systems of our bodies, and they make us feel good. So that makes us think it's actually a good idea to believe in the fairies, so to all intents and purposes, despite the empirical evidence, there are fairies at the bottom of the garden after all.

And we like that idea. It's nice. The fairies are nice too, although we never see them, but that's another thing that's nice about them. Some people might think we're mad for believing there are fairies at the bottom of the garden, but in fact we're just being human in wanting them to be there.

But more important than that, believing in fairies at the bottom of the garden is harmless. It might, indeed, improve the way we behave, make us more thoughtful or considerate, help us with the other contingencies of everyday life by encouraging us to tell our children delightful and elaborate stories about the fairies which, although a part of us knows that the fairies don't really exist, make our children laugh and therefore be happy, and that makes us happy too.

In fact, the only thing wrong with believing in fairies at the bottom of the garden is when you take that belief as the basis on which to build a priesthood which compels all your neighbours to believe only in the fairies at the bottom of *your* garden, and insists that the fairies at the bottom of their gardens are evil demons who will make their every action so evil as well that your fairies won't let your neighbours play with them after they've died.

And then you start killing your neighbours because they don't believe you.

*

The mad syphilitic atheist German philosopher Friedrich Nietzsche, whose career in philosophy came to a sudden halt when he couldn't stop himself cuddling a carthorse outside St Mark's Basilica in Venice, believed that the death of God was an enormity from which mankind could only recover by willing itself to stand in God's place. In *Thus Spake Zarathustra*, the madman in the marketplace who announces the death of God cries out to the crowd of bemused bystanders, 'How have we snuffed out the sun? How have we blotted away the oceans?'

I don't quite see it like that. Despite the best efforts of warring religions to stake a claim to a universalist monopoly, each one of them has always been part of a teeming multitude of rival ideologies, which include the kind of atheism I believe in, and the kind Richard Dawkins subscribes to. In the frequently mad marketplace of ideologies, an ecology operates, so religions come and go, mutate, adapt or become extinct.

I've come to believe in the rightness of my ideology for all sorts of different reasons, some of them rational and some clearly irrational. And although I thoroughly endorse my son Fred's and his friend Rory's rather brilliant comment, 'Saying atheism is a religion is like saying that bald is a hair colour', I square my belief in atheism with any contradictions the use of the word 'belief' might suggest by believing that religion is merely an ideology too, although one that has a dimension mine doesn't.

That's where I part company with the scientific secularists, who seem to base their atheism solely on the weight of verifiable empirical evidence, which can always be countered, and always is, by the argument that they've failed to factor in faith, just because they can't pin it down in the agar dish. That doesn't bother me, and shouldn't bother anyone else either.

Because I don't believe in God not because I can't, but because I don't want to.

And I believe that you should deal with the political dimensions of religion in political ways, whether it's over faith schools or Creationism or demanding special laws or special treatment denied to other equally sincerely or passionately held opinions, or any of the other aspects of religion's totalitarian imperative to control us and our lives. By and large, that political struggle is being lost by the religionists, and their current ferocity is, to a large extent, proof of the fragility of both their arguments and their position. And in many ways, and certainly in large parts of the world, the political battle against political religion is a case of pushing at an open door into an empty room, though that doesn't mean you shouldn't put your shoulder to the door anyway. Elsewhere, things are different, but again I'll be backing my ideology against theirs. And I think, and I hope, that I'll be on the winning side.

I believe that because, given a choice and given the opportunity, and all other things being equal, most people tend to prefer education for their daughters, control over their reproductive cycles, the chance to protect themselves from disease with condoms, the right to think what they want, over the political programmes offered by the various priesthoods, and 'belief', in the strictly spiritual sense, doesn't come into it.

That division between the two possible meanings of the word belief is probably a false one anyway. Although we assume that 'belief' in God implies an entirely different magnitude of belief than 'belief' in, say, the policies of the Liberal Democrats, I think that essentially they're the same, and have come to have different meanings over the centuries simply because the monopolists running the rival religions told us they did. No religion has ever had a global monopoly, and despite all the attempts to ensure brand loyalty (promise of paradise, forced conversion, death for apostates, torturing and burning heretics and so on), each one has existed in a marketplace. That's why hell is filled with demons who were once the gods of neighbouring tribes in Bronze Age Judea, placed there by the devotees of Yahweh as he muscled in on their territory to increase his market share. That's probably why St Paul was so proscriptive about homosexuality, even though the man who inspired the religion Paul subverted and corrupted never said a single thing on the subject, despite all the opportunities available to his editors at a later date: it was to mark Christianity (with its world-beating logo of a practically naked man being tortured to death on a tree) apart from the sexual tolerance of Hellenic paganism and the widespread acceptance in the ancient world of sodomy as a mark of priestly otherness and mystification.[45]

And that's why, even if God now came down in fiery splendour and proved beyond question his, her, its or their existence, I still wouldn't believe in him, her, it or them, because I'm unconvinced by the spiel and I don't like the way his, her, its or their brand takes a previous contingency from thousands of years ago and concretes it into certainty. I don't like the threats, the taunts, the patronising assumption to unchanging and unyielding rectitude and infallibility. In short, I don't buy the ideology. Like the Russian anarchist Mikhail Bakunin when he turned Voltaire on his head, I believe that if God existed, it would be necessary to destroy him.[46]

[45] Apart from being repellant, inhumane, inhuman and immoral (whatever the totalitarians may tell you), homophobia is also stupid. In his London Zoo lecture, Steve Jones observed that the optimum population size for a species like ours is roughly equal to the population of a city the size of Oxford, but thanks to our reproductive cycle and medical and scientific advances constantly being one jump ahead of nature, we're now beyond six billion and counting. In these circumstances, any group of altruistic, hard-working, well behaved, tax-paying and non-reproductive citizens should be applauded and encouraged, probably with medals and tax breaks. Unless, of course, you actively advocate a genocidal religious war to thin us out a bit.

[46] Bakunin's erstwhile friend, collaborator and possible lover, the nihilist Sergey Nechayev, more or less invented terrorism in its modern form, as a weapon to be used to overthrow governments, whereas previously it had been almost exclusively the preserve of governments themselves. Nechayev's avowed aim, in planting bombs and planning assassinations, was to destroy the power of the Church and the state. A popular slogan associated with the nihilists was 'Tear it down! It doesn't need rebuilding!' Despite what Tony Blair said about the 'existentialist' threat from jihadi terrorism, Nechayev and the nihilists' campaign really was existentialist, and kept the bourgeoisie of Europe cowering with terror indoors throughout the 1880s and 1890s at both the randomness and meaninglessness of the outrages, and the incomprehensible void at the heart of their political programme. Although they may have borrowed the nihilists' tactics, this is in contrast to the imperialist ambitions behind the terrorism of the Islamists.

And that's something else which divides my kind of atheism from Richard Dawkins'. He's on record, as a good empiricist, as saying that if the existence of God was verifiably proved to him to his satisfaction, he would be compelled, because of his respect for science, to 'believe' in him, her, it or them. He hasn't said whether or not that means that he'll consequently worship God, and Hitchens has kept schtum on the whole subject. However, it's just possible that if he ever were confronted with God, like on the desert island I mentioned in an earlier footnote, Hitchens would eat him, but obviously in an entirely non-sacramental way.

*

Without question many people will pick holes in what I've said. They'll say that God imbued us with the empathy, or that God created the universe in such a way as to make the development of our empathy either possible or inevitable. They'll argue that religion's political success and domination of a lot of the history of humanity we can ever know about proves, or at least suggests, God's sponsorship, and the crimes committed in his, her, its or their name are yet further evidence of humanity's massive shortcomings in comparison to God.

They'll also say that the shallowness and apparent emptiness of the lives of people living in post-religious societies proves that we need something like God to make sense of our lives, even though a main part of my argument is that's why we invented God in the first place, and anyway, that vacuity is less to do with the absence of God and more to do with the presence of the crass kind of consumerism with which governments have bribed us to buy our obedience and good behaviour. (On the whole, whatever price we eventually have to pay, this tactic is probably less objectionable than the only other tried alternative, typified by the kind of violent repression common to all totalitarian states, whether secular or theocratic. Making good the damage the rapacity of consumer capitalism causes to other people in faraway countries is a political struggle every bit as worthwhile fighting as the one against religion and all other totalitarianisms.)

And other people will say I've failed to take account of the levels of doubt many serious and thoughtful religionists wrestle with throughout their earthly lives, though I still don't 'get' why the existence of God should be the focus of their doubts, rather than his, her, its or their non-existence. And yet other people will say, with all sincerity, and equally sincere concern for my ultimate well-being, that my arrogance and my 'fundamentalism' are not only as bad as the religionists, but will also cut me off from the possibility of life after death and everlasting bliss. Others still will say my science is faulty, or my analysis of cognition is all to pot, or my jokes aren't funny, or I've got Time or evolution wrong.

Well, I don't really care. This isn't a textbook, even if I've chosen to go with my cultural conditioning by making it look like one by supporting my argument evidentially. But you and I know that this book is a rant. I may be certain in my rejection of God, or rather in my refusal to accept the notion of him, her, it or them, along with all the concomitant baggage, but I'm not demanding that everybody agrees with me, even though I'd obviously like that. But I'm not prepared to pay the price of forcing agreement on other people, beyond simply adding my voice to the beautiful Babel of human disagreement which, just as much as religion or keeping pets, helps define us as human. As to heaven, I'm with the great English irrationalist and absenteeist musician Syd Barrett who, days before he died in the summer of 2006, was asked by his sister what he thought about God and the afterlife. 'Do you know,' he's reported to have replied, 'it never occurred to me.'

And as for anyone who disagrees with what I've written so much they feel compelled to seek to kill me, all I can say is that that says more about them, and how far they've succeeded in stripping themselves of their humanity, than it says about me.

*

I think my whole position can best be summed up with a final metaphor, in which I'd ask you to look at religion as being like a human appendix. It once had an important function, when our evolutionary forebears subsisted on a different diet, but because things always move on for many of us it's now just vestigial. In other words, it no longer serves any useful function. It doesn't bother us most of the time, though of course it becomes a problem and can actually kill us when it gets inflamed. Then again, we stand as much chance of dying if we elect to have it removed, like many children who underwent appendectomies in the 1950s and 1960s because the medical orthodoxy of the time said the organ had no functional use, and was better out than in. But even if we're hours away from death, and our survival depends on its removal, you may still die, either because the surgeon's incompetent, or the anaesthetist's hungover or the recovery ward is fatally filthy because of the incompetence of bureaucrats or the budgetary constraints imposed by an ideologically motivated government.

But, because I'm human and not entirely or even mostly rational, that's not an end to it. I might easily work myself up into a fury of irritation about my appendix, either because I'm enraged that I'm part of a wasteful and random system of life that leaves my body cluttered up with useless old rubbish, or because it's taking up space which could have accommodated something far more useful. You know, like a flying gland, or one of those organs that killer whales have that emit a sonic pulse which stuns their prey. These frustrations are irrational and pointless, but they do mark me down as human, with a fertile imagination along with all the other qualities with which I've been equipped to cope with the realities of a life which is, as far as we'll ever be able to tell, both random and meaningless. And if you find that bleak, what on earth did you expect?

You could, of course, comfort yourself with the idea of your body rotting down to its component minerals in order to compost the future lives of creatures that will evolve to replace us, although I doubt that that's really any comfort at all. But it's about as comforting as a line Luis Buñuel borrowed from a Carmelite monk he'd once met and used for satirical and surrealist effect in several of his films: 'If only everyone prayed every day to St Joseph, everything would be fine.'

But both approaches are more immediately comforting than the inevitable reality, which is that we will become extinct in our turn, either through our own folly or because we fail to adapt in time to meet changing circumstances. Apart from the rest of creation breathing an intense sigh of relief when we eventually die out, it's worthwhile wondering what God will do then. Will he, she, it or they weep for our demise and the curtailment of the supply of fresh human souls to worship him, her, it or them? Or will he, she, it or they be content to catalogue the dead souls now clogging up heaven and hell? Or bide his, her, its or their time until another species evolves with a large enough cerebral cortex to glimpse the concept of God, and start the whole thing over again? Most likely, however, our gods, along with our art and culture, will die out with us, as you'd expect of something that has its origins entirely and exclusively from within ourselves.

In the meantime we comfort ourselves with what we can grab, or what we can make up. But however uncomfortable we may find the recognition of the meaninglessness of life, if our existence had any purpose or meaning beyond what we, as humans, imbue it with from within ourselves, we wouldn't be able to grab any kind of comfort at all, because we wouldn't need to. We'd simply function like cogs, without cognition, because an organised scheme of things would have no need for us to have to do anything else. And so we wouldn't have imagined such an infinite range of possible explanations, or such a massive diversity of templates for our lives, or any of the other beautiful, amazing, extraordinary things that mark us out as the wonderful yet terrible creatures we are.

And that's a final reason why I'm an atheist, and why I continue to be deeply irritated by our continued surrender to religion. It closes off so many possibilities of both thought and action, and makes us yearn for, or often impose, the same limitations on other people. In short, religion turns us into lackeys.

Or, if you prefer, religion makes us all God's running dogs, but where the dog is eternally being wagged by its tail.

*

I don't particularly like dogs, and I never have. Nonetheless, I own one. More correctly, my family owns a small brown poodle called Ginger, whose acquisition I grudgingly acquiesced to, in spite of my deep misgivings. I think that my dislike of dogs is because of their subservience, the way they're so compliant in being trained to do the stupidest things. I also know that they have this propensity because they've evolved from animals that, like us, hunted in packs, which also explains the extent to which they, too, display empathy. From this arises all those qualities we like about them: their loyalty, their obedience, their compliance when we invest our love in them as well as our ability to control

them when there is so little else we're able to control. Then
again, we've spent thousands of years selectively breeding
them so they'll comply with what we require from them.

On the whole, though, I prefer cats. I like their self-
reliance and the obvious contempt they hold us in as they
demand more food and then destroy our furniture. Maybe
it was that aloofness which made the Ancient Egyptians
turn cats into gods, although it's more likely that this was an
obvious way to venerate, and thus protect, these useful
creatures who controlled the vermin infesting the grain
stores along the Nile. My fondness for cats (which I'm sure
doesn't get even remotely close to deification, though I can't
swear to that) probably springs from whatever it was that
also made me a satirical cartoonist: in other words, a dislike
for authority and obeying orders and a respect for anyone or
anything else who manifests the same propensity. But each
to his or her own, and because my family wanted a dog, I've
got one too.

That said, my unhappiness was so great after her arrival
that Ginger almost went back to the breeder in Purley
whence she'd come. But she didn't get sent back, and for an
interesting reason. One evening my wife came home from a
particularly unpleasant and distressing dental appoint-
ment, in pain and in tears, and none of the family was able
to offer her any kind of adequate comfort until Ginger
curled up in her lap and fell asleep. It was quite clear that
the dog was able to either generate or reflect enough
unquestioning love to make Anna feel better, and had
revealed that my wife had within her a previously
undetected Dog-shaped hole. That was quite enough for me
to change my mind and let Ginger stay. And because my
wife and children loved the dog, I began to love her too.

Quite soon, despite making it absolutely clear that I could
not be expected to either feed or walk the dog, I was doing
both. I'd also insisted that there were no circumstances

whatsoever in which I'd scoop her soft, sloppy shit from the public streets, although I was soon doing that too, even though each time I did it I ended up gagging with the dry heaves for about five minutes afterwards.

To give her her due, Ginger is a nice dog. She's friendly, affectionate, reasonably obedient, and although she smells a bit she's unquestionably cute and fluffy, as I discover anew each morning when I take her for a walk in our local park. Toddlers and tiny children in pushchairs scream with delight when they see her, and stretch out their tiny hands to try and touch her, and gaggles of teenage girls walking to school fall to their knees to worship her, making that strange but immediately recognisable and highly articulate human vocalisation, the slightly nasal, falling and rising intonation which means 'This thing I'm seeing is simply *adorable.*' They do this even as she jumps up at them with her muddy paws and tries to lick their faces with her doubtlessly pestilential tongue. But I never have the heart to tell the little girls to pull themselves together and stop acting so irrationally.

And because I love Ginger because I love my family, I'm protective of her too, and worry about her well-being and safety, and try to defend her from the multitude of perils that life might bring her way. These include the dogs of other dog-owners in our park in South-East London, and I'm always having to second-guess the next possible move of some slavering hellhound baying and bounding towards us over the football field or round the swings. As often as not, the owners of these curs are lost in conversation with their friends, or on their mobile phones, and either don't notice or don't care that I'm trying to fend off their pets, grabbing my dog from some rottweiler's jaws or shaking a labradoodle off Ginger's back or my thigh.

So, although I don't much like dogs, because of human love and empathy I now often find myself behaving quite

disgracefully, possibly even insanely, in public as I scream
at the top of my voice at total strangers: 'WHY DON'T YOU
KEEP YOUR FUCKING DOG UNDER CONTROL, YOU
STUPID IRRESPONSIBLE BASTARD!?!'

But as with dogs, so with gods.

Blame the owners.

Appendix A

'A Little Dog Cried' by Jimmie Rodgers

This is the story of a little orphan pup
Some people don't believe that it's true
But I'll tell it the way it was told to me
And I'll leave that up to you.
Some say he was a shepherd dog
Or maybe only part
A mongrel breed by birth perhaps
But a thoroughbred at heart
One day he wandered down the road
Lonely, tired and unfed
He was willing to trade his poor little heart
For just a pat on the head
He came upon a stranger in a garden, I understand
Who gave him bread and water and the puppy licked his
  hand
Well he thought he'd found his master at last
And at his feet he lay
An angry shouting mob came by
And they took his master away
He saw them tie his master's hands and take him before a
  judge
Well they tried to shoo the puppy away
But the little guy just wouldn't budge
He saw him stumble and fall three times

As he followed him down the road
He saw him stumble and fall
Because he carried such a heavy load
Then lightning struck and thunder roared
And all the world grew dark
And it's been said that only those who stayed
Heard a little dog bark
Well you may not believe it
It doesn't sound true, I know
But a little dog cried when his master died
On a hill a long time ago.

Appendix B

Henry (Harry) Marten

Henry Marten deserves far more recognition than he gets, both for his role in the English Revolution and in his own right. His loose morals, his drinking and his wit all serve to make him easily the most attractive of the English regicides, and when he was signing Charles I's death warrant he started an ink fight with Oliver Cromwell, neatly conflating Marx's dictum about History repeating itself as farce. His father, a judge and far more moderate politically and personally than his son, also deserves his due, if only for this wonderful destruction of the principle of precedent, be it in law, religion, scholarship or anything else, delivered as part of an opinion in favour of hearing the Petition of Right in 1628:

> We must not tie and bind ourselves by all that is done before. I have gone over the Thames in former times on foot, when it was all on ice, but that is no argument to persuade by, to do the like now because I did it once.

Marten also understood the absurdity of trying literally to put the clock back and recapture some illusory 'Golden Age', an attitude typified by, among many others, Islamist plans to re-establish the caliphate. He also, like his father, rejected the common belief that certain ideas are simply impossible because they defy the pre-existing order of things.

Throughout the period leading up to the English Civil Wars, the political debate between privilege and prerogative, order and freedom, was fuelled by the belief that ancient English liberty of the kind enjoyed by the pre-Conquest Anglo-Saxons had been perverted and suppressed by what many called the 'Norman Yoke'. Once again, we see how a political agenda is promoted through the evocation of a grand narrative which appeals to a largely illusory historical precedent of the kind that Marten's father abjured. Marten himself made many speeches in the House of Commons in which he talked about 'Freedom restored'. But when other MPs challenged him, saying that he knew as well as they did that the kind of liberty he was advocating had probably never existed, he came up with a typically witty response. It was, he said, like a man born blind who suddenly is able to see in later life: we always describe this as his sight being 'restored'. In other words, liberty is the default setting of humans, even when temporarily if enduringly denied to them. That you can apply the same template to Saul of Tarsus' temporary blindness before his sight was restored and he accepted the Revelation of Christ in no way invalidates Marten's argument.

Towards the end of his long imprisonment, Henry Marten wrote the following acrostic epitaph for himself, which strikes me as a beautiful summation of how to live as an atheist, and how you'll die:

Here or elsewhere, all's one to you, or me,
Earth, air, or water grips my ghostless dust,
None knows how soon to be by fire set free.
Reader, if you an oft tried rule will trust,
You'll gladly do and suffer what you must.

My life was spent with serving you and you,
And death's my pay, it seems, and welcome too;
Revenge destroying but itself, while I
To birds of prey leave my old cage and fly.
Examples preach to the eye; care then (mine says)
Not how you end but how you spend your days.

Appendix C

Just to tip my cap to my day job, here's my drawing of
God . . .

Appendix D

International Animal Noises

HEBREW

DOG	Hav hav
CAT	M'iau
MOUSE	None (they say mice don't make noise)
FROG	Kwa kwa
HORSE	A snore
COW	Moo
PIG	Jews ignore pigs
DUCK	Ga ga ga
CHICKEN	Koo koo ri koo
LION	None. Apparently they just watch the lioness with satisfaction and yawn
SHEEP	Meh

DUTCH

DOG	Waf
CAT	Miauw
MOUSE	Piep
FROG	Kwaak
HORSE	Hinniken
COW	Boe
PIG	Knor knor
DUCK	Kwak kwak
CHICKEN	Yoktoktok
LION	Brullen

SPANISH

DOG	Guau
CAT	Miau
MOUSE	Iii
FROG	Croac
HORSE	Hiiii
COW	Muuu
PIG	Oink
DUCK	Cuac
CHICKEN	Pio pio
LION	Groarrrr

GERMAN

DOG	Wau wau
CAT	Miau miau
MOUSE	Piep piep
FROG	Quaak quaak
HORSE	Brrrrr
COW	Muh muh
PIG	Oink oink
DUCK	Quackquack
CHICKEN	Kikeriki/ Gack gack
LION	Roooooaaaaaaaaarrrrrrrr

NORWEIGIAN

DOG	voff
CAT	mjau
MOUSE	pip
FROG	kvekk
HORSE	knegg or possibly vrinsk
COW	mø
PIG	nøff
DUCK	kvakk
CHICKEN	klukk
LION	brølte

GREEK

DOG	waf waf
CAT	niau
MOUSE	iii
FROG	kouax
HORSE	eeeeeeeee (cannot make the throat sound when typing)
COW	mououou
PIG	oink
DUCK	cuac
CHICKEN	papapapapapapa
LION	wouaaaaa

BRAZILIAN PORTUGUESE

DOG	au au
CAT	miau
MOUSE	None
FROG	None
HORSE	hiiii
COW	muuu
PIG	oinc
DUCK	quack
CHICKEN	cocoricó
LION	uaua

FRENCH

DOG	ouaf ouaf
CAT	miaou
COW	meuh
DUCK	couac couac
CHICKEN	cocorico (roosters only)